MORE PRAISE FOR *SOMEDAY I'L*

Someday I'll Miss This Place, Too is a stranger-in-a-strange-land memoir, the story of a newly minted California-educated lawyer who finds himself doing legal aid work in the remote Yukon Kuskokwim Delta. The year commitment stretches to twelve. To say the author comes of age there is both a given and an understatement. His profound respect and compassion for the people he serves, mostly troubled Yup'ik Alaskans, haunts both him and the reader. Branch invokes in me a curious sense of *fernweh*, a feeling of longing for a place I have never been. This is as Alaskan as any book we have, both culturally significant and deeply moving.

— David Stevenson, author of four books, most recently
High Places, Sacrifices, Mysteries and *Forty Crows*

Someday I'll Miss This Place Too

DAN BRANCH

Cirque Press
Copyright © 2021 Dan Branch

Published 2021 by Cirque Press
Sandra Kleven — Michael Burwell
3157 Bettles Bay Loop,
Anchorage, AK 99515

cirquejournal@gmail.com
www.cirquejournal.com

Book design by Emily Tallman, Poetica
Interior photographs by Susan Oshida, Dan Branch, and Ed Page
Front and back covers: A very groggy Dan Branch at the finish line of the 1984 Kusko 300 dog team race.

Print ISBN: 978-1-7375104-5-1

CIRQUE PRESS

This book is dedicated to Susan, my wife, and to the memory of
Professors Eva Saulitis and Sherry Simpson, mentors now dead.

This book is also dedicated to the Yup'ik people of Southwest Alaska,
whose grace, kindness, and patience with my stumbling still makes
me homesick for Bethel and the Kuskokwim River. Readers should
understand that while many of these essays share my impressions of
Southwest Alaska from 1976 until 1989 when I moved away, they do
not try to paint a picture of current life on the river.

CONTENTS

DISCLAIMER

I was in the Yukon Delta as an attorney, so identifying information of former clients has been omitted, and dialogue attributed to them did not occur during interviews. The names of all of the characters in these narratives have been changed except for the mushers mentioned in "Because I Asked," the Amik Family mentioned in "You Can't Go Home Again," and Susan, my girlfriend during much of the narrative period and now my spouse. To preserve client confidentiality, I've changed the identifying information of former clients. For the same reason, the dialogue attributed to clients in child abuse or domestic violence cases is inspired by, but does not reveal the statements or facts that I remember from client interviews.

PART ONE

Bethel

Dan and two little friends sitting on the front steps
of Alaska Legal Services Office, *Winter, 1978*

Welcome To The Bush

With faith of the ignorant, I hand the Wien Air Alaska agent my boarding pass and enter a blue-carpeted tunnel connecting Anchorage to the plane taking me to Bethel, in Western Alaska. It's late September 1976. Outside the airport, birch tree leaves yellow in air cold enough to serve as winter in my native California.

Cigarette smoke fills the cabin within seconds after the captain extinguishes the no smoking signs. He keys his mic as the 737 drops like an express elevator to let us know that we are experiencing a little turbulence. Faith slightly shaken, I follow his advice to keep my seatbelt fastened but order a double whiskey from the slightly swaying flight attendant before she pushes her tinkling drinks cart further down the service aisle.

The whiskey soothes but then opens carefully closed doors in my mind. Fears tucked behind rationales or diversions slide out with panic in tow. It will be below freezing when we land in Bethel.

Before leaving California, I dreamed about the wild and romantic life on the last frontier, a place where people travel between villages by dog sled in winter and paddle skin kayaks in summer. The VISTA bureaucrat who issued me survival gear in Anchorage shattered the dream. Skiffs with outboard motors replaced kayaks fifty years ago, dog teams are just for racing or camping. "You'll need this heavy parka for the next nine months," he said while handing me a magenta-colored monstrosity stuffed with down. "The wind chill will be sixty below." Next came a battered

Coleman camp stove and lantern to use when the power goes out. "The guy you're replacing needed these last winter when the town power plant burned down." I guess the VISTA-crat expects it to burn down again.

The 737 cabin seems hot, but most of the passengers still wear their parkas. I want to remove mine or at least slip the felt-lined Arctic Pac boots from my sweaty feet, but I don't want to stand out. One of the passengers might live next door to me in Bethel or even be my new boss. While I bake in down and wool felt, a guy sitting across the aisle leans over and shouts, "You're the new schoolteacher?" Without waiting for my answer, he booms, "Maybe you're replacing that girl the college hired out of California. She flew in last week on an evening flight, pranced around the airport in high heels for two minutes, and flew back to Anchorage on the return flight." Red-faced, with a voice that carries back to the smoking rows, he assures me that I won't be finding him at the college. He operates a D-6 Cat. I can smell the lubricant oil from one of those big-bladed earthmovers that soaked into his Carhartt overalls.

An hour into the flight the captain announces our gradual descent into Bethel. I give D-6 a weak smile and look beyond him to a window. It frames a plain broken by thousands of small lakes and one large river. D-6 interjects, "That's the Kuskokwim. It runs by Bethel and some other downriver villages like Napakiak before dumping into the Bering Sea. Without it, there'd be no salmon, no way to travel in the summer, no town." Within a few weeks I will know that except for a small commercial fishery and fur trapping, the area has no industry. Some Yup'ik people work for cash with the non-Native transplants in schools, government offices or construction. Most families subsist on harvested fish, game, and wild plants.

Having reacquired my attention, D-6 ramps up my discomfort level with a lunch box of Bethel horror stories—like how all the new residents spend three weeks bedbound with a dysentery-like disease called "the Bethel crud." I say a small prayer for my health as the jet touches down and its reverse thrusters drown out his voice. After the plane bounces to a halt, I bend low over the middle seat to get my first look at Bethel. It's flat, what I can see of it, and dotted with diminutive leafless shrubs. Except for a small sheet-metal terminal, I find no evidence of man or his civilization.

After the captain turns off the fasten seatbelt sign and welcomes us to Bethel, we exit out the rear stair door. Smiling like a person who will not be spending the night in Bethel, the flight attendant warns me to take care on the icy tarmac. The warning sinks in just as one of my boots slides forward and I fall on my rear.

I duck walk into the terminal where people pretty much ignore me until a baggage guy slides open two sheet-metal doors, exposing the luggage cart on approach to the terminal. Locals in the air terminal will comment, in a language I do not understand, about each deplaning stranger. I imagine men and woman comfortable in their culture pointing at my ridiculous magenta parka and saying, "That funny-looking guy's wearing a coat the color of fireweed flowers."

Soon, two men in dark blue Wien uniform overalls toss our luggage onto a plywood platform. I look for my framed backpack and cardboard box among the suitcases, duffel bags, and countless cases of beer. Mr. D-6 grabs his luggage, which includes two cases of beer. I ask him how he can bring booze into a dry town, and he tells me, with a look of pity, "The town is damp, son, not dry. You can import liquor, you just can't sell it."

After extricating my now slightly bent backpack and box of survival gear, I head outside. A line of cabs—all low-clearance navy blue Chevy sedans—idle in the dark. Sliding into the back of one marked "Kusko Cab," I ask the driver, a young Yup'ik man, to take me to Dave Jonah's place in Subdivision. A friend of the lawyer I will be replacing at the legal services office, Dave offered to house me for the night. My driver says in a quietly determined voice, "Wait." I do.

During the delay I study the cab's sagging seats decorated with cigarette-burn craters. The interior smells of tobacco smoke and something I would learn to associate with Pine Sol disinfectant. A Christmas tree shaped air freshener hangs from the driver's rearview mirror over a glowing radio airing a news broadcast in Yup'ik.

I am about to try another cab when Mr. D-6 slides into the seat beside me. He's followed by three other passengers who announce their destinations as they enter. A young Yup'ik woman with toddler says, "Housing 32" as she quietly settles into the front passenger seat. "FAA," announces the man with a government-issue briefcase. Mr. D-6 asks for a drop off across the slough.

We stop first at the fenced-in FAA compound where the government man pays the three-dollar fare without tip before walking over a dormant lawn to a 50s-style clapboard-sided house. D-6 tells me, "Take a good look at that lawn. It's the only one in town and it will turn dead brown in a week." We pass a series of similar houses, all looking as if lifted from their native Kansas suburb then plopped onto the tundra by aliens.

Back on the main road, the cab passes a crude wooden ark. I ask the driver whether it had floated there on a record flood. "Joke," he answers without a smile. D-6 tells me that a local fish buyer built it during a very rainy summer. "People were getting a little bushy," he says—an explanation wasted on me.

I can just see the lights of downtown Bethel when the cab's dispatch radio crackles, "Go trailer court fourteen." The driver backtracks, and then navigates through a geometric maze of identical trailers to number fourteen, where he stops and honks. Everyone but the toddler watches a beautiful young Yup'ik woman in sweatshirt and jeans stamp out her cigarette and trot over to the front passenger door. She waits for the mother and child to make room before saying, "Disco." I watch the dim reflection of the cab radio dial in her raven-black hair all the way to Dave Jonah's house.

Dave lives in Subdivision, an inspiration of the new city planner. The city council approved his grid of rectangular lots laid out in straight lines. With a good sense of community standards, they rejected his zoning proposals, so people can build anything they want in Subdivision. We pass an octagonal log house flanked by residences constructed from semi-truck freezer vans. A fair-sized "A" frame house sits across the street. I can't see any street signs or even house numbers so I ask the driver how he can find Dave's house. He tells me that his dispatcher has a map marked with the name of everyone in town.

If there was a real estate agent in Bethel, he would have called Dave's place a rambler. That's real estate talk for a box with tin roof and fancy plywood siding. After paying the driver and taking one last look at the Disco-bound woman, I wander around the outside of Dave's house looking for the front door. In deepening darkness, I stumble on a path of two-by-six boards half mired in mud that leads past a foul-smelling bucket to the door. Burdened with gear, I mount the front steps and kick the door. Dave, a middle-aged white man, opens it and says, "Oh, the new VISTA."

After dragging self and gear into his living room, I ask Dave how he knew that I was the new VISTA. "It's the pink parka," he explains in a low smoker's voice. "No one would pay money for it."

A ragged brown beard shot with streaks of gray hangs from Dave's tired face. He has a full head of hair but apparently spends little time keeping it under control. An aggressive strand curves just above his bright blue eyes. He teaches English at the town's tiny college.

Dark walnut paneling lines every wall of Dave's place, making it more a series of connected caves than modern living space. Naked bulbs hanging from the white acoustic tile ceiling light each room. After I tell Dave that his front room furniture seems nice, he says that he ordered all his furnishings from the Sears Catalogue. I settle into a brown velveteen armchair, sip on the mug of coffee he hands me, and notice, with a little relief, that he has a phone. He points proudly at the plain black rotary dialer and says he had to wait 14 months to get it. "It's a party line, but since everyone in the party is known by voice, no one hogs it for long."

Silence settles over the house while I concentrate on its unique smells: acrid dust, number one grade fuel oil fumes, and the honey bucket bouquet of pine-scented disinfectant partially masking the stench of human waste. Smiling with contentment Dave says, "Great place, it even has a shower."

The Anchorage-bound jet rumbles through a climbing turn over Dave's house. Reaching his hand into the cupboard, he takes down a quart bottle of Wild Turkey and says, "There goes the freedom bird. Now you're stuck here until at least tomorrow." After he medicates my coffee with the high proof liquor, I silently vow to stay in Bethel a good deal longer than that.

While the booze relaxes both of us, Dave talks about Bethel.

"You're lucky you weren't here when the town had a bar named the Sugar Shack and it was legal to buy booze. They called Bethel the Las Vegas of the Kuskokwim since so many people came here from their villages to party. It wouldn't have been so bad if Bethel weren't the hub city. The folks living in most of the fifty-six surrounding Native villages still have to fly through Bethel to get to the Lower 48 or even Anchorage.

We got the hospital, troopers office, and the only large stores in an area the size of Kansas."

After taking another sip of Wild Turkey, he tells me I am now a minority. "You have just joined the small number of white people living in Yup'ik territory." He should have said that I had just moved to a place without any familiar cultural anchors.

Dave finishes his drink and says good night. I drag my stuff into his spare bedroom and dig through the box looking for a recently purchased book about the people of the Kuskokwim River.

I am too embarrassed to tell Dave that I am here to keep a promise I made to a professor at Berkeley. After my Native American studies class had visited a BIA boarding school near Pyramid Lake, Nevada, the professor asked each of us what we intended to do for Native American people. The school visit made me willing. Even though it was sunny and pleasant outside, the kids had all slumped in chairs or lay listless on their bunks. The place sucked the joy out of my classmates and me, like it had the kids. Knowing I would attend law school after graduation, I promised to spend a year providing free legal services in Indian country. Someday I will wonder if fulfilling my promise to the professor made me just another missionary helping indigenous people disappear into the great American mixing bowl. I want to do good in Bethel but I can only help people survive the American legal system, not gain independence from it.

I will dip drinking and washing water from a barrel, live on tasteless Sailor Boy pilot bread, maybe even lose teeth from scurvy. I won't even be able to develop a drinking problem because the town banned liquor sales.

Since most Bethel housing lacks indoor plumbing, I will relieve myself in a galvanized bucket and live with the smell until it is emptied by the honey bucket man.

Then there's my work for Volunteer in Service to America (VISTA) at the Alaska Legal Services Office. I'll have to handle cases involving things I know nothing about like domestic violence, child abuse, traditional lands claims, and hunting rights. Just months out of a San Francisco law school—still waiting for the bar exam results, with only the thin experience of three months at a Mission District legal aid office, my big victory there bringing unemployment benefits to a man who wore a superhero's cape to every job interview—I will be expected to represent real people with real legal problems.

Although I wouldn't mention it to any Viet Nam war veterans, I hope that my service here will help me feel less guilty about completing school while they served their country in that mistake of a war. Years away from Bethel, after reading war memoirs like Tobias Wolff's In *Pharaoh's Army*, I will cringe when remembering that I considered my VISTA year as penance, clothed as service to America, for any encouragement given to the Viet Cong by my presence at anti-war rallies.

While trying to fall asleep in Dave's spare room, I remind myself that I am only staying in Bethel a year, just long enough to fulfill my promise. Then I will return to San Francisco hoping that this detour to Bush Alaska doesn't hurt my chances of securing an associate attorney position with a downtown law firm.

Dave is already at work when I wake up. Fighting through my usual morning fog, I wander the little house until stumbling into the bathroom. There's a small porcelain sink and prison-box shower that both drain directly onto the ground beneath the house. A "toilet" sits between the two. Ignoring the smell allows me to appreciate its clever design: a hard-plastic toilet seat and lid attached with a hinge to a twelve-inch-high white metal cylinder within which rests a handled galvanized bucket, now half full of human waste. A three-inch pipe vents most of the smell outside. This is my first experience with a honey bucket. Last night I followed Dave's advice and relieved myself outside. I lift the lid and sit down, welcomed to the bush.

Young Yup'ik dancer at Bethel National Guard Building,
Winter, 1977

Mamterillermuit, Village
of the Smokehouse People

Before the Moravian missionaries arrived on the River from Pennsylvania, the Yup'ik people of Western Alaska migrated from one seasonal camp to another, efficiently harvesting salmon and other fish from the river as well as useful land animals, sea mammals, berries, and wild greens. They used the place where Bethel sits today for smoking and drying salmon. Today it is called Mamterillermuit, Village of the Smokehouse People. The Moravians settled here because their ocean-going transports could not go any farther up river. Like a magnet, the mission attracted trading posts, schools, a post office, the hospital, jobs, and the Yup'ik community that holds the majority of Bethel's population.

The pre-Moravian people made beautiful art, practiced a loving faith, taught and treated their children with respect. They did not need lawyers or money. Today, thanks to the doctors that arrived after the Moravians, they have longer life expectancies but face a myriad of new problems.

In 1971 the Yup'ik people received millions of dollars and title to millions of acres of their traditional homeland in a settlement with the U.S. Government. The deal required them to form business corporations that would own the land and manage the money. They held shares in the corporations. Their leaders spent more time as corporate directors than hunters or fishermen. Yup'ik people needed legal help to fight for state and federal financial assistance, seek state court resolution of their family law issues, or contend with the legal fallout from alcohol-related problems. They must have appreciated the efforts of Alaska Legal Services lawyers, who provided the bulk of legal help on the river. Their name for "lawyer" translates as "one who helps."

In 1976, three thousand people lived in its plywood mansions, shacks, apartments, and dwellings made from converted shipping containers. I lived on food stamps and my $500 monthly stipend from Volunteers in Service to America (VISTA).

The town had one judge, three grocers, no bars or liquor stores, and three miles of road. Only an informal seawall of junked cars and trucks protected it from river erosion. I swelled the membership of the Bethel Bar Association to eight. Five of the other members worked with me in the Alaska Legal Services Office. We served cash poor people living on the Yukon and Kuskokwim River Deltas, a place the size of Kansas. The region suffered from high unemployment and poverty rates. Our clients subsisted in Dena'ina towns on the Yukon River, in villages where people spoke Yup'ik, or in places on the Bering Sea coast where they used a variation of Yup'ik called Cup'ik.

The Californian

My first day working for the Bethel Alaska Legal Services office, I met my mentor attorney Mike, two secretaries, a paralegal, and two other VISTA lawyers, but not my supervisor. "The boss is traveling," Mary, the office paralegal, told me, "He is always traveling." Since he led the team forcing the state to build high schools in all Alaskan villages, our boss had good reasons to be on the road. Even if he watched over my shoulder every work day, he wouldn't have been able to help me learn the rules for the world I had entered at the Bethel Airport. Without a basic understanding of Yup'ik culture, I could do more harm than good with my legal skills. That made Mary just as important to me as Mentor Mike or our supervising attorney.

Mary came from a village on the Bering Sea coast about halfway between the mouths of the Yukon and Kuskokwim Rivers. Her long black hair framed a round, almost always smiling face. As well as English, she spoke Cup'ik and the dialect of Yup'ik spoken on the Kuskokwim. She was a patient translator and a kind but sometimes blunt cultural advisor. Years of trying to stop non-Native lawyers from offending Yup'ik clients had taught her that the Yup'ik way of non-confrontation did not work with us.

My first week on the job, after helping me interview a client from the Johnson River, Mary said, "You kassaakaq (White person) lawyers have no patience—never wait for people to tell you what they want. Learn to drink your tea until they are ready to talk." This prevented me from asking why her translation of my six-word question took five minutes or how she reduced the client's ten-minute-long response in Yup'ik to "Yes."

In early November, Mike, the lawyer I was replacing, walked into the office kitchen, days before we were to fly to the Bering Sea village of Hooper Bay. He had promised to teach me the ins and outs of village travel and to introduce me to my new clients. I had just topped off the teakettle with water dipped from the fifty-five-gallon barrel that the city water truck filled every week. Mike watched me place it on the office hotplate before saying, "Branch, there has been a change of plans." As the hotplate burner turned orange he explained, "I got a boondoggle to Miami, chance to get some sun and heat before winter sets in, good legal training too of course. So, you'll have to go to Hooper Bay on your own." I digested this bit of news while dunking a bag of Lipton's tea in a mug of boiling water. *Why not? How bad could I screw up?*

Mary, the office paralegal knew how many ways I could screw up. The day before my flight to the village, she sat me down on the office couch and said, "Iitu Avayaq (branch with big eyes), listen to me. Don't you embarrass us in that village. If someone offers you something to drink, you say, 'Quyana (thank you)' and take it. If someone offers something to eat, you thank them and eat it. If they invite you into their house, you

Wien Air Alaska flight unloading freight at
Hooper Bay Airport, *Winter, 1977*

sit down and wait for them to ask you for help. Don't start talking first like some kassaakaq."

I reviewed Mary's lesson at eight the next morning while I waited to board a Wien Air Alaska flight to Hooper Bay. The blue and gold Twin Otter's overhead wings rocked in the wind as the ground crew removed a canvas cover from each of its engines. Wanting to use a flush toilet in the terminal, something I couldn't do at home or the office, I walked toward the bathroom and then heard, "Wien Air Alaska's flight to Hooper Bay, Chevak, and Scammon Bay is now boarding."

I finished my business, walked onto the runway, and got in line behind a dozen passengers—a couple of young male school teacher types (white/ bearded/blue jeans/expensive down parka/beaver hat) and members of Yup'ik families. The older Yup'ik women wore hooded parkas covered with bright, cotton-print fabric. Wolf ruffs trimmed their parka hoods. The young women had sweatshirts and tight jeans. Most of the Yup'ik men wore one-piece, insulated snowmachine suits. I sported a wool balaclava collapsed into a watch cap, thick wool pants, and a magenta-colored puffy parka. After I wore the pants every day of my first Bethel winter, Carmen, the best-dressed secretary in the office, gave me a new Yup'ik teasing name that meant "big eyes branch who wears funny old pants."

There was no flight attendant to check our tickets or help us find seats. I took the last empty one, which was next to the port side engine. The pilot and co-pilot, each looking like they had just made Eagle Scout, walked through the cabin to the cockpit. Before buckling in, the pilot pointed out the emergency exits, and said, "Anybody not going to Hooper, Scammon or Chevak should get off the plane." When none of the passengers moved, he closed the coffin-shaped cockpit door.

Something exploded inside the port engine, which then belched smoke and sputtered to life. Like the props on the plane that flew Ilsa Lund and Victor Laszio out of Casablanca in the 1942 Humphrey Bogart movie, the Twin Otter port propeller rotated faster and faster until the engine roared. Only the plane's wheel brakes kept us from moving. The pilot cut back on the throttle until the engine purred. A new explosion brought the starboard engine to life. The plane didn't take me to freedom in Lisbon but across a hundred miles of open tundra to Hooper Bay. There English was the second language. I was unknown.

None of the passengers appeared concerned about being flown by children over a trackless morass of watery tundra. I ignored the metal seat bar pressing into my shoulder blades and looked for houses or someone in a boat who might spot us if we crashed. An hour after takeoff, the Twin Otter banked into a turn and descended toward the tundra. It slowed, drifted and then plopped onto a long, military-grade runway before rolling to a stop in front of a tiny log building with a "Wien Air Alaska" sign. After shutting off the engines, the pilot slid open the cockpit door and said, "hooper dooper." He lowered the rear door and bounced down the steps. The passengers stirred, grabbed their carry-ons, and left the plane. When I was sure that all the other Hooper Bay passengers had deplaned, I eased down the plane's steps as a battered pickup truck stopped near the plane. The truck driver, a Cup'ik man from the village wearing blue Wien Air coveralls, ignored us. The co-pilot dumped our luggage on the runway and with the help of the guy in blue coveralls, loaded pop, whiskey, groceries, and mail sacks into the truck.

I could just make out the village a mile down the road. Most of the passengers hopped on fat-tired ATVs. Others climbed into the bed of the pickup. Not wanting to seem like a pushy white guy, I waited for everyone to drive off and walked to the village.

There were no farmer's fields, grazing caribou, no ocean or bay view. I couldn't figure out how people could find enough to eat on the great flatness that radiated out from the village. I had the road to myself, even the part that led past houses on the edge of town—a scattering of plywood-sided ranches suspended above a bog on wooden posts. *Were people inside those homes laughing at the funny-looking kassaakaq?*

Mike, the lawyer I was replacing, had told me to stay at the jail if they had room, so I wandered around until I found it in a wheel-less trailer marooned near the BIA school complex. "You going to jail?" a smiling boy asked. He laughed until a young Yup'ik man in brown and tan mufti came out of the trailer.

"Go away you kid!"

Inside, I introduced myself and asked if I could spend the next few nights in his facility. He handed me a mug of coffee and pointed to a can of evaporated milk with a lid pierced in two places by a beer can opener.

"Most kassaakaqs only stay one night. You can sleep here unless we get busy. May happen. They brought in some whisky on the plane you came here on. You can leave your bag there. You with the BIA?"

"Legal Services."

I should have told the cop that Mary ordered me to stay at least three nights to give our clients a chance to decide if they trusted me. But, I didn't want to lose the smug feeling I had from being considered different from other kassaakaqs.

"Legal Services? You want me to put an announcement on the CB?"

"Sure."

He grabbed a microphone, waited until no one was talking over the channel people used to start a conversation, and spoke in Cup'ik, the dialect of Yup'ik spoken here, salted with a few words I could recognize like "Bethel," "legal services" and "kassaakaq lawyer." A woman broke in and had a conversation with him. When he was finished, the policeman said, "I told them they could see you at the city offices. A lot of people go there because it has the only telephone in the village. That was Agnes, the city clerk. She said it was ok for you to go there."

Before I left, he told me that he grew up in Hooper. I said I had moved to Bethel a few months ago from California.

"California. You must be cold," he said and turned up the jail's thermostat to 80 degrees.

Following his directions, I walked up a boardwalk trail to an unpainted plywood house with a "Hooper Bay City Offices" sign nailed over the door. Inside someone answered a phone, said, "wait," picked up the CB microphone and shouted, "Dundu, go twenty." This effort to have a private conversation failed when everyone with a CB turned their radio to channel twenty. The phone clerk told Dundu he had a call. Two minutes later, a guy rushed in, picked up the phone and said, "Ii-i" (yes).

Agnes gave me a coffee as strong as the one I had just downed at the jail. This time I thought about adding some evaporated milk but took it black. She did paperwork and sometimes answered the village phone. The caffeine made me nervous so, after an hour, I decided to hunt for clients at their houses rather than wait for them to come to Agnes's crowded office. I wasn't sure if they would want her to know that they needed my legal help but I couldn't think of any way to find them on my own so I asked Agnes for directions to their houses. She told me that the first man on my list was in Bethel but should come back soon. She knew that the next person, a woman, worked at the school but could see me at her house after five. Agnes thought the third person should be at home and directed me back to the odd set of pastel ranch houses I had passed on the way into town.

Because she thought that it might close soon and Hooper Bay didn't have an eating-place like Bethel, Agnes told me to shop at the Sea Lion Store before seeing my client. Non-perishables filled its well-dusted shelves. I found Sunny Jim jam, canned stew, spaghetti, Vienna sausages, and Sailor Boy pilot bread (big, round, dry crackers) like my father brought on backpacking trips when I was a kid. They even sold self-opening tins of deviled ham and turkey meat sandwich spread. Since the jail didn't have a kitchen, I selected pilot bread and some canned turkey meat to spread on the large crackers. I would have bought some fruit or raw vegetables but the store had nothing to ward off scurvy. The residents got their vitamins and nutrients from seal meat and other wild food they hunted or gathered. On a later trip. when I came down with a cold during a visit to the village, an eighty-year-old grandmother would nurse me for days with seal meat soup rich in vitamin C.

After shopping, I stood in line behind people paying for their purchases with unemployment or government welfare checks. Each received as change a combination of cash and previously negotiated government checks made out in smaller amounts. The clerk told me that the store couldn't keep enough money on hand to cash checks so, with the nearest bank in Bethel, they had to treat the cancelled checks as cash. It was the only way to keep money flowing in the village. He seemed happy to receive my tiny infusion of greenbacks.

Martha Campfire, a young woman dressed in a Hooper Bay High sweatshirt and jeans, opened the door of my first client's house as I started to knock on it. She offered me kuuvviaq (coffee), which I took, and pointed to a plate stacked with pilot crackers next to a tin of Crisco shortening and a butter knife. She seemed to be alone. In the twenty minutes before she spoke again, I memorized the house's interior.

The Campfires had a bathroom but since the house lacked running water, they kept the toilet taped shut and used the tub for storage. Three small bedrooms opened onto the common area where I sipped my coffee. Four-inch gaps had opened between the ceiling and the bedroom walls. In the future, I would work on a lawsuit to make the state replace this house and the others in the subdivision designed for people living in Arizona. A large, oil-fired cook stove provided the only heat. Steam rose from the enamel coffee pot simmering on the stovetop. Clumps of dry beach grass hung on a clothesline stretched across the room a foot below the ceiling. Their odor of dried lawn clippings mixed with that of boiled coffee, fuel oil soot, and the fresh sea smell of rendered seal blubber (seal oil). Some of the dried grass had been used to weave the bottom of a small basket that sat on the edge of the table. When she finished it, the woman who gave me coffee would sell the basket to the hospital's gift shop on her next trip to Bethel.

I sat up in my chair when an elder, silver haired and slightly stooped, walked out of one of the bedrooms carrying a shoebox. He wore a thick, buffalo-plaid shirt and wool pants held up by suspenders. Plaid carpet slippers covered his feet.

"Cama-i, quyana, hello," he said as he handed me the box. Martha said, "This is Peter Campfire. He wants you to look at the papers in the box and say if any of them are important."

I could tell from the dates on the envelopes that no one had looked over Mr. Campfire's mail since Mentor Mike's last visit. The shoebox contained months of junk mail, government paperwork, and letters from the village and regional corporations in which he owned stock. The corporations were the vehicles mandated by Congress to implement settlement of Native land claims. The corporations held title to the land received in the settlement and managed the village's cash settlement, part of which the village corporation had used to build the Sea Lion Store.

I told Mr. Campfire to ignore the Publishing Clearinghouse flyer that assured "occupant" that he or she had won a prize. He didn't want a new suit sewn by a Hong Kong tailor visiting Anchorage, so I tossed the tailor's ad in the trash. I helped him respond to the request for information from the state Division of Public Assistance and hoped that they would not cut off his old age payments because his response was four months overdue.

I could have been in the Bethel office drafting a class action complaint to prevent the state from setting unrealistic deadlines for public assistance information requests rather than explaining how magazine sweepstakes work. But my mail triage had lifted a burden from Mr. Campfire. He was disappointed to learn that the Publisher's Clearing House prize team would not visit him, but relieved that I defused all the bombs that had lurked in his shoebox. If Public Assistance cut him off for not answering on time, I could make full use of my education.

Since I had accepted Martha's many offers to refill my coffee mug, I had a caffeine overdose when I left the Campfires. A sharp ringing hurt my ears. I forced myself to move without haste to the door, shake Martha's hand, and ask for directions to the home of my next client, the one with a job at the school. Martha had to repeat the directions twice because I couldn't concentrate on her words the first time.

Three grade-school-aged boys walked with me along the way to my next client's house.

"Where you from?"

"Bethel."

"No, where you really from?"

"California."

"Iillake, you must be cold. You got kassaakaq food? We want to try."

I showed them my box of pilot bread and they ran away laughing. Despite my caffeine distress, I didn't mind their teasing. In the office, Mary was always teasing me. When she smiled afterward, I knew that she meant no harm. Her teasing made me feel at home. The kids' teasing seemed like a sign of acceptance, like they thought I was another person, not just a kassaakaq. It made me want to see life through Yup'ik eyes and understand the language. I longed to belong, have people call out my name, ignore my whiteness and the uncomfortable way I moved in my unfamiliar Alaska clothes. But expecting to be back in California within the year, I knew I would never be more than another kassaakaq 'crat. I just hoped that I would do more good than harm before leaving the tundra for a middle-class life in the Lower-48.

My next client handed me a mug of black coffee after I sat down at her Formica table. It looked just like the one at the Campfires' house, and I wondered if they had ordered from the same catalogue. "I am all coffeed out," she said while making a pot of java. "But all you kassaakaqs love to drink coffee."

Setting a mug on the table in front of me, she asked, "Where are you from?"

"Bethel."

"I mean before."

"Oh, California."

"Nice. You must be cold."

While she turned the heat up on her oil range, a diapered toddler, moving as stiff-legged as a candidate for hip surgery, walked up and steadied himself with a hand on my knee. He swayed back and forth like a clump of basket grass but kept his brown eyes on my blue ones.

"Maybe he likes you."

When I smiled and said, "Hi," the little guy tumbled back onto his diaper and looked stunned. His mother snatched him to her lap before he could cry. He turned away and leaned against his mom's shoulder. She rocked him while she asked me to help her grandfather write a will.

"You must be flying back to Bethel in the morning. Maybe you could see Apa (grandfather) next time you are here."

"I'll be here for a few more days."

"Really!"

After making arrangements to meet her grandfather the next day, I left so she could cook dinner. I said goodbye to the toddler, who was playing with a plastic parrot toy. He gave me another soul gaze. *Are mine the first blue eyes with which you have shared a stare?*

I knocked on the jail door and, when no one answered, walked in to find it empty. The furnace jets burned high even though it felt like a summer day in the desert. I wanted to crack a window or turn down the heater but didn't think it was my place. It didn't occur to me that the cop left the thermostat turned up so high so the Californian would not catch cold. After stripping down to pants and undershirt, I spread canned meat over a couple of pilot crackers and ate while listening to Cup'ik chatter on the CB radio. The CB conversations continued into the evening and provided background noise while I stretched out to read on a jail cell mattress.

It was hard to concentrate on my book with so much caffeine cruising around my brain. At 10:00 p.m. I jammed my head into the top bunk when an air raid siren sounded. Footfalls on the boardwalk pounded past the jail and I heard the cop yell, "Curfew. Go home you kids." He stuck his head in the door and said, "Maybe I'll see you later if there is any business tonight." I thought that this was more teasing but I still spent the night on half-alert in that overheated building, ready to hop up when the first drunken prisoners appeared.

After a breakfast of Pilot Bread and water, I continued to meet clients but drank only tea. That night, the policeman lowered the jail thermostat before he left for the day.

On my last morning, I asked a client for directions to the Wien Air mail plane agent's house so I could book a seat home to Bethel. He asked his son to take me there. I followed the boy along boardwalks through the old village, which sat on a grassy hill above the tundra. He entered a small arctic entryway crowded with nets, foul weather gear, and a galvanized washtub full of cold water and small, black fish with heads like salamanders. "Black fish," my guide said as he pushed open the door into the house. "We eat them."

Sun poured into the front room through a multi-paned window. It formed a pattern of shadows and light over a seal stretched out its back on the kitchen floor. In a tone I would have used when his age to tell the milkman that Mom wanted an extra cottage cheese, he said, "He just got the seal. She is going to clean it."

The seal's nose pointed at a wall covered in funeral cards, each with a romantic rendering of a saint and the birth and death date of a deceased family member. Among the holy cards hung crucifixes that once sat on top of coffins and a picture of Pope Pius XII, who had died in 1958. While I waited for the mail plane agent to wash off the blood of hunting, his wife knelt beside the five-foot-long seal and made an incision from throat to anus through its dappled fur. This exposed the seal's layer of white blubber. She worked with a wicked-sharp ulu. The knife had a rocking horse curve on the cutting surface and a narrower flat side to which the mail plane agent had fastened a wooden handle. Her sure hand made the minimum cuts necessary to remove the seal's fur without damage. Later she might sew it into an airtight poke (bag) to store dried salmon soaked in seal oil that she rendered from the seal's blubber.

The friends I left behind in California months before wouldn't have recognized the hippie lawyer, who tried to follow Mary's cultural advice while bumbling through a Cup'ik village, and taking for granted the kindness shown by villagers through offers of coffee, tea, and teasing. I longed to join the new culture into which I dogpaddled. I accepted without question the evisceration of a seal beneath a family's wall shrine without grieving the seal's loss even though its face retained a dog-like charm in death. It didn't even seem strange to watch the bloody deed while waiting to book an airplane flight.

The agent let me ride in his truck to the runway where we waited in silence for the mail plane. On the way, I spotted wire-mesh nets set in narrow streams for needle and black fish and the arrow shaped formation of south-flying geese. The other passengers arrived on ATVs right as the Twin Otter landed. A half dozen people got off the plane. I waited for everyone else to board and took the only open seat. After stops in Chevak and Scammon Bay, the plane headed back to Bethel.

I looked out the window at a spot on the horizon and thought about my visit the previous day with Mr. Blue. He wasn't in the house when I arrived but his daughter had said, "You from Legal Services? He will come." I drank tea and waited. After cataloguing the contents of their living room, I searched outside for a distraction. Their kitchen window looked out over a table-flat expanse of tundra, featureless except for something moving near the horizon. When it grew in size, I knew it was heading toward me. It appeared to lumber from side to side like a bear, not move with the purposeful stride of the wolf. In minutes I could see that it was a man carrying a shotgun. Soon after I spotted the two geese, feet tied together, that hung around his neck.

What I took for a lumbering gait was a flowing shift of feet from one tussock to another. Even when the hunter was close to the house, he didn't smile, wave, or give the impression that he could see me through the window. I was surprised when he entered the arctic entryway, hung up the brace of geese, and sat down at the table.

"This is my father, Simeon Blue. He wants you to help."

"Ii-i, yah," he said and asked in Cup'ik for tea. I found it easy to wait in silence for Mr. Blue to finish his tea, to keep my pen and yellow pad out of sight until he asked for help.

Dan driving his dogsled team on a rare day when
they all worked together, *Winter 1977*

Bargain Dog Team

One very damp September day in 1977, a day when even the Bethel cabs couldn't avoid getting stuck in the town's muddy streets, fellow legal aid lawyer Robert and I waited for my girlfriend Susan to pick us up at the Legal Services Office. If not stopped by the road mud, she would drive us out to the FAA colony site where a man named Ray was offering to sell his Mackenzie husky female and her six pups for $150. When I called him on the phone, he admitted that the Mackenzie husky was big, but pretty loveable. The pups were about six months old. Ray offered to throw in a sled, feeding pans, seven plywood dog houses, and 100 pounds of dog food for no additional charge.

I would have never have been able to buy Ray's dogs, if our boss at Legal Services hadn't finally found enough money to keep my friend and I working in Bethel. Robert and I were finishing our first year of lawyering as VISTA volunteers. Legal Services was having trouble finding money to pay us next year's salary. I was about to head back to California when the corporation's administrator called from Anchorage. To convince Robert and me not to leave, he offered to pay us $1000 a month. We had been surviving well on a $500 monthly stipend from VISTA. The new salary would double it. We could easily come up with $75 each to pay for the dog team and have enough left over for dog food, harnesses, and a gangline to attached the pups to the sled.

Susan drove around the swampy holes in our street and onto the one paved road that connected Bethel and the airport. Three miles later, she parked the car next to Ray's FAA house. After serving us coffee and cookies, Ray led us out to his dog pen. On the way, he mentioned that Tukluk, the mother dog, was half wolf. This made me nervous as we approached her. Then she rolled over on her back and held her feet in the air like a lap dog.

Ray claimed that mushing legend Joe Redington, Sr. had raced Tukluk in one of the Fur Rendezvous heats in Anchorage. Neither Robert or I had attended Anchorage's Fur Rendezvous Race, but we wanted to believe Ray's description of our future lead dog. He said we could build a great team with Tukluk and her pups, even though he had to admit that Tukluk weighed 97 pounds. If she had raced with Redington, she could lead her pups to victory for us.

Neither Robert or I realized that Tukluk weighed almost 60 pounds more than a well-built sled dog. We had no idea how slow she would move. We believed Ray's Joe Redington race story and ignored the sluggish way that Tukluk waddled around her dog house.

Ray claimed that he had paid the owner of a male malamute $400 to be the sire of Tukluk's puppies. That made Robert and I believe that we could to build a winning team with her litter of pups.

To put us into an even better mood, Ray showed us the old wooden sled he was throwing into the deal. After one of the sled runners had shattered, he cut both of them away from the sled stanchions and replaced them with heavy wooden cross-country skis. Ray admitted that it wasn't the best sled in Bethel, but he said its lack of grace was compensated by its charm and strength. "It should get you through the winter," he assured us.

After our dog food supply order arrived from Anchorage, we took possession of our new dog team and drove them to the end of 6th Avenue. In a year or two, the city would extend to 6th, opening up more lots for building new houses. But the day our pups arrived, the road ended near our driveway. We formed a village for them by dragging their tiny plywood houses to a dry spot near the end of the avenue. Then, we drove a length of steel pipe next to each one. Tukluk and her pups were secured to the pipes with a long chain. I thought they might struggle or complain about their new housing situation, but they shook their tails and barked as we filled their feed bowls with a dinner's worth of high-protein kibble.

While not lawyering for Legal Services, Robert and I sought knowledge from the town's other dog mushers. We spent each night reading and re-reading dog mushing guides. One recommended the use of German words to command the dogs. We could not snap out German, so we decided to use English words like "Hike" to start, "Whoa" to stop, "Gee" when we wanted the leader to turn right, and "Haw" to turn left. We tried to teach our dogs the commands while on individual walks.

The first big snow storm hit Bethel that November. It covered the snow machine trails leading out of town. Excited, Robert and I dragged the sled gear and dog harnesses out to the dog yard. It didn't take us long to connect the gang line to the sled. Assuming that she wouldn't take off, we hitched Tukluk to the lead dog end of our unanchored sled and went back for one of the pups. Tukluk dragged the sled away up Sixth Avenue. It took us the rest of the morning to track her and the sled down on the other side of town.

After a month of similar mistakes and near disasters, we learned how to harness each dog and hitch them to the anchored sled's gangline. We still spent more time untangling the dogs than mushing. If they weren't tangled, they were trying to chase birds or rabbits. None of the dogs seemed willing to lead. Whichever one we put at the front of the gangline would pull the team in any direction other than the one we ordered.

These runs provided great entertainment for our neighbors each weekend. But after six months, the dogs actually started to work together as a team. By then, Tukluk had been forced to take a position near the rear of the gangline. Junior, one of her pups, took lead. He was nearly as stubborn as his mother. But he humored his humans by occasionally responding to commands.

Robert, a much better dog musher than me, started dreaming about the annual Iditarod Race. It ran each year from Anchorage, over 1100 miles to Nome. By then we had improved our team by finding homes for Tukluk and some of her less helpful pups. We replaced them with veteran dogs bought from local Iditarod mushers. But Robert wanted better. One night, while drinking tea at my cabin, he told me that Joe Redington, Sr.

had promised to lend him a large team of reliable sled dogs. They would give him a good chance to finish the Iditarod race. Robert still wanted to take Trotski and some of the better dogs with him to fill out his new team.

We had been in Bethel long enough to adapt some of the Yup'ik ways of non-confrontation. Rather than yell or argue that Robert was being a jerk, I said "OK." He was the man on fire, not me. In 1983 he would finish the Iditarod in 27th place. The following year, guided in large part by Robert's advice, I'd run the Kuskokwim 300 dog race from Bethel to Aniak and back.

✳

I think I would have gotten out of the sled dog business after Robert and I broke up if not for Bilbo, a long-legged dog with thick fur and a collie shaped head. He was Tukluk's brother. Another dog musher took Bilbo off Ray's hands before Robert and I met Tukluk and her pups. Like Tolkien's hobbit character Bilbo Baggins, Tulkuk's brother had courage, cleverness, and compassion.

One day I got a call from Bilbo's owner. He told me that he had to give up his dog team and wanted to know if I'd take his lead dog. I said, "Sure," not knowing why he wanted to pass a good dog onto me. If he knew that Bilbo had some bad health problems, he didn't tell me.

Later that afternoon, I picked up Bilbo and hitched him up to the sled as a lead dog. He immediately improved my ability to drive the dog team out of the yard and down a nearby tundra trail.

Bilbo never had to bark at or bite a misbehaver. When I shouted, "Hike" all the team dogs would follow him down the path. He seemed impeccable until we were heading back to the dog yard after a long, downriver run. Five miles from home, he collapsed onto the tundra and had a seizure.

I set the sled anchor and ran to Bilbo. He was still shaking, so I disconnected him from the gang line to keep him from choaking. Ten minutes later he dropped into a deep coma.

Bilbo growled at me when he woke up, giving me a suspicious wolf stare. Then he ran off.

A normal acting Bilbo was sitting outside his plywood dog house when I returned the dog team to the yard. He wagged his tail as I unharnessed the other dogs. I think he even yelped out some happiness when I reattached his chain and gave him a little head pat. I left the yard shaking my head. I was dreaming about running the Kusko 300 next year. I wouldn't be able to if Bilbo kept having seizures.

Bilbo had several more seizures while leading the dogs down the trail. Each time he returned to his house before us. I was about to start training one of his teammates to lead. Then I heard a story on our NPR station about hypoglycemia, a condition that could cause weakness, confusion, and coma in humans. Since the problem for humans could be controlled by diet, I started carrying chunks of frozen salmon for Bilbo on training trips. He never had another seizure.

For the next nine years, Bilbo lead my other seven dogs through overflow water, into wind that would freeze my exposed skin in minutes, and around teams of sled dogs that snapped at us when we passed. More than once, he brought us home through heavy snow storms that reduced visibility to zero. He was always the smartest member of the team.

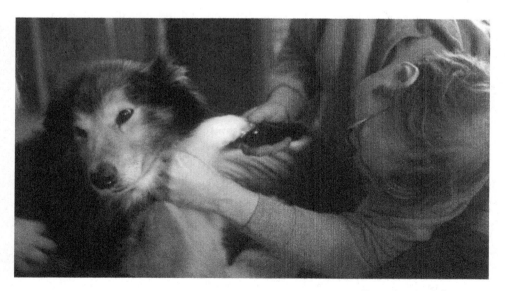

Dan trimming Bilbo's paws

The Skiff

This is a story about bad judgment, unwarranted good luck, knowledge from stumbles, and a leaky skiff.

On a Kuskokwim River beach in front of Bethel, Alaska, a bearded white man dropped a six-gallon gas can onto the planks of his creek-robber-gray skiff. With the help of me, a Volunteer in Service to America (VISTA) who had expressed an interest in buying it, he pushed the skiff into the river current. As water flooded up between the floorboard planks, he said:

"She will leak a little bit at first but that should stop when the plank seams swell tight. You won't even have to bail. Just pull out that plug there under the motor when she's on step, and the water will drain out."

I did not know that a skiff skimming on the river's surface while under power is on step. I sat on a middle seat in the old boat, glad that I was wearing waterproof boots.

"She's a little tough to start when she hasn't run for a while."

Two inches of water sloshed over the floorboards by the time the outboard came to life. The seller sat near the motor, grabbed the tiller arm, and pointed the boat upriver. I felt engine vibrations through my seat as the skiff rose up on step as if lifted by strong hands.

Minutes after the seller pulled the drain plug, the floorboards were almost dry. I watched the riverside willows fly past as we cruised on flat calm water into Straight Slough. Late afternoon sun bounced off the

Swapping out a new prop blade

slough and lit the white tent cabins of the fish camps they passed. Women in calico kuspuks hung raw, dark-red strips of king salmon meat on horizontal drying racks. I imagined myself drinking tea in front of my own fish camp tent as the woman who loved me hung up strips cut from fish I had netted in the skiff. The woman would always be kind, the skiff dry, motor faithful, and there would be plenty of salmon. The dream blinded me to the jets of water that shot up through the floorboards every time the skiff bounced through a boat wake.

After the bank opened Monday, I took possession of the skiff. The next weekend, I invited my girlfriend then, and now wife, Susan, and some others on a boat ride to Napakiak—a Yup'ik village twenty river miles downstream from my home in Bethel. The village's plywood-sided store was the only place on the river that sold Ghirardelli chocolate.

We had a good day for a skiff ride. The sun shone but did not bring wind to ruffle the river with chop. Sunlight brightened the water to the hue of milky tea. Just as we approached Napaskiak, not Napakiak where they sold good chocolate, I noticed a line of small rapids on the port side of the skiff. In seconds I learned that water running over a shallow sandbar raised such rapids. That is when the outboard slammed into a sandbar and snapped up and out of the water. The transom board, to which I had carefully tightened the motor clamps, cracked. The top half of the board left the boat with the engine attached. Later, I would learn to secure the motor to the skiff with a chain or strong rope. I grabbed the rubber fuel line, which soon parted from the motor. With hose in hand, I watched the motor spiral around and around, each revolution bringing it closer to the water's surface as the boat continued downriver. Seconds later it lay partially submerged on the sandbar. I plugged the drain hole but couldn't stop the water from leaking up between the skiff's floorboards.

Without the flood tide we would have drifted toward the Bering Sea until sunk. But the tide checked our progress and pushed the boat upriver to the motor. With the help of one of the passengers, I lifted it out of the shallow water and clamped it onto what was left of the transom. I thought myself lucky to have recovered the motor but would later wish I had left it on the sandbar and let the boat sink, if possible, without loss of life.

We would have rowed to shore if I had brought oars.

I loved Susan and liked two of the other four people in the boat—another VISTA and his girlfriend. These friends smiled reassurance as the water level inside the boat rose. In soft North Carolina tones, Steve, the other VISTA, said, "At least we still have the gas can and fuel line. I would have never thought to grab the fuel line."

I choose to name Steve's girlfriend Tasha, not to avoid confusion, but because I was working my way through Tolstoy's Russians at the time of the motor's attempted escape, and she found joy in most experiences, like Tolstoy's Natasha Rostova. I won't bother to name the other male passenger or his scowling girlfriend. They did not especially like me and had invited themselves on the trip for the chocolate. They did not smile reassurance. They pouted and said things that most people would consider ungracious. Fear of drowning can bring the worst out in some people.

The tide shifted while I reattached the motor. Now nothing checked our downriver drift. Even though we floated toward the Bering Sea in a sinking skiff with at least two people who thought I was a moron, I believed that everything would be okay. The teller of this story, a decades' older version of myself, would like to note that if placed in a similar situation today, I would not think it was okay to be floating toward the Bering Sea in a sinking boat with a malfunctioning motor, but that would be a lie.

I reattached the fuel line to the motor and pulled on the starting rope, but the engine gave no sign of life. Then, a metal skiff with two Yup'ik men left the beach in front of Napaskiak. Their motor started on the first pull. The Napaskiak skiff driver brought it alongside my sinking boat. While the other Napaskiak man held the gunwales of my skiff, the driver climbed aboard with a sparkplug wrench in his hand. Without speaking or showing any emotion, he lifted off the engine cowling. He had a deeply tanned face and hands but white skin flashed each time one of his shirt cuffs slipped back as he worked. Five minutes later, when the old Johnson was idling smoothly, he left the boat. Whether he could hear my "thank you" over the sound of the engine was never clear. I felt like a rescued child. I would feel that way after each of the many times a Yup'ik person saved me from frostbite or other consequences of bad decisions made through ignorance or overconfidence.

A wise person would have turned the skiff upriver and returned to Bethel before something else could go wrong, but there was little wisdom in the skiff and by then everyone was hungry for fancy chocolate.

If I had not continued on to the village after the motor's attempted escape, I might have been able to drive the skiff back to its home mud bar in upper Brown Slough. But, the whole time we were in the village the tide ebbed, draining the slough to a bare trickle. The flood tide wouldn't refill it with enough water for passage until three the next morning.

After filling their pockets with fancy chocolate bars, everyone returned to the skiff, which managed to deliver them to a Kuskokwim River beach in front of Bethel where I left it until high tide.

That night I stayed up reading Solzhenitsyn's *A Day in the Life of Ivan Denisovich* so I would be awake at 2 A.M. to return the skiff to its Brown Slough home. While I read, I listened to KYUK, the Bethel public radio station, until 11:00 p.m., when it played the Alaska Flag Song and went off the air. Then, I tuned in Radio Free Moscow for the classical music.

After Rimsky-Korsakov's Scheherazade, I listened to one of the "Boris and Natasha" vignettes:

RFM announcer, warm voice, speaking with smooth American accent:

"Welcome American friends to Moscow's beautiful Kremlin Square. I think I see our friends Natasha and Boris walking this way."

(Sound of a man and woman walking across an empty room in leather shoes)

"Boris, Natasha, how are you? Would you like to say something to our American friends?"

(More studio footsteps)

Woman with an American TV anchorwoman voice:

"Hello my American friends. If your politicians, all chained dogs of imperialistic capitalist exploiters would only stop blinding you with propaganda, you would know how happy the Soviet people are with their lives and their beloved leaders."

I suspected that this Natasha was not named after Tolstoy's Natasha Rostova. Suddenly feeling patriotic, I turned off the radio before hearing from Boris. My cabin was only a short bombing run from the Soviet Union's Siberian bases and the parabolic antennas of the U.S. Air Force's early warning system dominated the Bethel skyline. It was only midnight so I returned to *Ivan Denisovich* as the protagonist scoured his gruel bowl with a bonus scrap of bread as dense as the first volume of *Gulag Archipelago*. I felt as cold as I had each previous time I read the book. That night I might have also felt jealous of the luck Denisovich enjoyed and the skillful way he repaired the power station walls. I, who had purchased *Denisovich* because it was short, Russian, and didn't come with a chart of the thirteen names of all the major characters, thought I should have substituted a collection of Chekhov's plays.

At two in the morning, I walked down Main Street toward my boat and wondered if any other American streets with that name were covered in mud that could suck the shoes off your feet. I managed not to lose my boots as I moved past open patches of tundra, the Moravian Church and the RCA tall communications tower. I saw no cars or people. At the river I turned right and walked toward the skiff. It was dark so I had a hard time finding the right path. A careful person would have brought a flashlight, but I didn't own one. I tripped on a plastic bucket that reeked of pine-scented disinfectant and human waste, relieved that I did not step in it. The beach smelled of old fish, acrid river silt, and DEET bug dope. The latter floated off a human silhouette, which turned out to be Steve.

"I thought you could use a hand."

I only mumbled, "Let's get this over with," as I placed the anchor in the skiff and shoved off into the river current. Steve sat in the bow and scanned the darkness for floating tree trunks and the entrance to Brown Slough.

While reading about St. John of the Cross thirty years later, I would identify that Brown Slough boat ride as a "dark night of the soul." But if pressed by conscience, I would have to admit that I experienced no conversion that night.

Steve and I motored slowly around hairpin turns where tangles of willows tried to pull us from the skiff. The eerie but beautiful sounds made by diving snipe warned us to turn back. More stubborn than wise or even brave, I ignored the little birds. I continued up the slough, sometimes slamming the skiff's bow into a willow tangle, other times getting it stuck in sucking mud. Always, the mosquitoes bit.

The sky lightened to predawn gray as I nosed the skiff onto its mud bar parking space. I picked up the gas can from the small lake that had formed in the bottom of the skiff and carried it and the oars up Sixth Avenue to my army-green plywood rental and said goodbye to Steve. I was too sleepy to tally up the few lessons learned on the way to Napakiak. But, I never again hit the sandbar near Napaskiak or let anyone ride in the skiff who thought I was an idiot.

The skiff spent much of that summer on the mud bar. When I did drive it down the slough, I always turned upriver, not down, so I could row home when the motor broke down. After the slough ice melted the next spring, I set a wheelbarrow in the skiff and motored down slough to Gus's house. The eighty-year-old Yup'ik man, a Russian Orthodox deacon, and part-time carpenter had agreed to caulk the skiff's seams.

I used the wheelbarrow to deliver the old forty-horse outboard to Swanson's Marina for a tune-up. I lingered in the marina showroom to look at the shiny new thirty-five-horse Evinrude motors that could offer easier pull starting and worry-free operation. Then a staff attorney for Alaska Legal Services, I considered buying one of the motors, but my new salary barely disqualified me for food stamps, and I felt a misplaced loyalty to the old dancing motor.

Gus had the skiff floating dry in the slough when I wheel-barrowed the rejuvenated motor up to his house. Looking into my eyes, the elder said, "You are a young man. Buy a tin boat. This will get you through silver salmon season, MAYBE." The old man's words faded from my memory the next day after I brought the skiff up on step. The river had already broken up and it ran high and thick with pans of rotting ice and driftwood. People in other skiffs roped thirty-foot-long white spruce logs, towed them to shore, and tied them to stout willows. After the water dropped, they would cut the logs into firewood for the next winter.

I planned to ride my old skiff in future river rodeos if I ever bought a home heated by wood.

When the king salmon passed through Bethel in June on their one-way trip to their spawning beds, I tried to catch one with a three-hundred-foot-long drift net that I had borrowed from a messy friend. I managed to untangle and then set the net perpendicular to the current like a real fisherman but caught only an undesirable dog salmon. That night, confident that it no longer leaked, I parked the skiff on a slightly protected beach near Mission Road. I ate dog salmon for dinner and packed for a work trip to the upriver village of Aniak, where Susan and I would eventually live.

While I had tea with an Aniak man who needed legal help to get a commercial fishing permit, a southeast storm moved out of the Aleutians and slammed into Bethel. Forty-knot winds whipped up waves on the river that broke on the beach in front of my skiff. The storm had reached Aniak by the time I boarded a Harold Air's twin engine Piper Navajo bound for Bethel. I wondered why only one other person, a young Yup'ik woman, left the crowded, passenger's waiting area to board the plane. I am now embarrassed to confess that this was only one of the many times that I had boarded a plane in weather that had kept almost everyone else on the passenger list home drinking tea. I relaxed a little when the woman, the pilot's girlfriend, smiled as she buckled into the co-pilot seat, but my nervousness returned when she clutched the pilot's hand while he taxied the plane onto the runway.

The Navajo rocked in the thirty-five-knot wind as the pilot ran through the preflight checks. After kissing his girl for what I told myself was luck, the pilot slammed forward the double throttle, and the plane leaped into the air. The plane dropped two hundred feet like a broken elevator and then recouped the loss, slamming my head into the cabin ceiling. "Trust me," the pilot mouthed to his girlfriend as she clutched a now-full vomit bag.

I managed not to throw up on the flight to Bethel, and the plane landed in one piece. I took a cab directly to Mission Road, leaned into a strong wind and headed toward a low bluff that should have offered me a view of the skiff. I saw only waves slamming onto a now empty beach. A guy dressed head to toe in rubberized rain gear from Norway staggered up and shouted over the wind noise, "Good thing we moved our boats before the storm."

I should have felt fortunate to be rid of the old skiff with its grumpy motor. But lacking wisdom, I felt loss. After the storm, I walked the riverbank looking for places where it might have washed ashore. Riding downriver in a friend's boat, I found the skiff, nose down, near Napaskiak. The friend said, "Sand in the bow of your skiff must be keeping it upright." Grabbing the prop, I could feel it shudder each time the bow bounced on the river bottom. Soon the skiff would pogo its way into deep water and drift out to sea. Denying the skiff a Viking death, I held on to the outboard as my friend drove his boat onto a nearby beach. I experienced almost all the stages of hypothermia after dropping into the river to secure the boat to a beachside willow.

Was it a hypothermic euphoria or a shepherd's joy I felt between bouts of head-rattling shivers on the ride back to Bethel? Today, calm in a warm room, I grieve the skiff's lost chance for an honorable end.

"Here comes the sand man," the Marina mechanic said when I arrived to pick up the old forty horse. He handed me a bucket half full of river silt taken from the outboard and a three-hundred-dollar repair bill.

The skiff and motor never recovered. Carefree was a word I never used even to describe rides on sunny days over calm water. Unless I could begin and end a boat ride on a high tide, I kept the skiff on the Brown Slough mud bar near my cabin. During berry picking in July and August, I only worked patches near a broad beach. I carried extra tools so I could remove the flywheel of the old motor and clean its points when it refused to start. When that stopped working, I finally replaced the cranky Johnson with a new Evinrude 35-horse motor.

By the time the silver salmon began running up river in August, I had saved enough money to buy a used 16-foot metal boat from an Indian Health Service dentist. The sage green tin boat was light where the old skiff was heavy. It had a drain plug, but I didn't need to use it to empty the skiff after it went on step. *Gus, I am a young man with a dry tin boat.*

In late August that year, after several hard frosts had sweetened the low bush cranberries but before everyone with a skiff and money for boat gas headed upriver to hunt moose, I gave the old skiff away to a Yup'ik fishermen. He just needed the boat until just before freeze up when he would abandon it in a back channel of Brown Slough. It was a socially acceptable way to rid yourself of an old boat. A month after, Brown Slough and the Kuskokwim River froze over. A freak southeast storm moved through Bethel two weeks later, breaking up the ice and flooding Brown Slough. The old skiff, freed from its icy confinement, floated on the high water and came to rest on the snowmachine trail that linked my sled dog yard with the trails I used to train my team.

When the snow arrived that year, I gathered together dog harnesses and a gangline for securing five dogs to my sled. Bilbo, my collie-like lead dog, erupted from his plywood house and led the others in a chorus of howls and whines. They went wild when I connected the sled to the old snowmachine I used as an anchor. The level of excitement rose a notch each time I hitched another dog to the gangline. They jumped and strained against their harnesses to free the sled.

I wrapped lengths of chain around my sled runners to make it harder for the dogs to pull it over the icy trail. I jerked a quick release on the anchor line and said a prayer. The team shot across Sixth and Seventh Avenue and onto the glare ice covering the Brown Slough trail. I didn't spot the old wood boat frozen athwart the trail until Bilbo had leaped over one of its gunwales. I would like to tell readers that I had never before failed to check the slough trail before the first dog sled ride of the year. But I never did such a safety check, even in the years after I bought the tin boat.

The team dogs followed Bilbo up and over the skiff. If I had not tried to use my sled brake to slow them down and instead just held on, the sled would have made it across the skiff intact. But I did depress the brake—a piece of sharpened angle iron bolted to a four-inch board attached to the sled with a door hinge. It caught on the gunwale and broke off. The chains unwrapped when the sled hit the ice on the other side of the boat. Without a brake or the chains to slow them down, the dogs accelerated. They galloped for a half an hour before slowing to a trot. I didn't find the gallop refreshing.

After the dogs slowed, I thought I might know the offending skiff. I called out, "Come Haw Bilbo" and the lead dog made a "U" turn. On the return trip I spotted my rotten old skiff lying across the trail.

Falling

In September, a week after I moved to Bethel, one of the government nurses invited me to a party at her cabin. I learned in half an hour that most of the other guests spent too much time together. One would finish a sentence started by another. Then, they would both roll their eyes. I could barely follow the conversations. Their English words had somehow morphed into sets of code, unbreakable without translation by the speakers or their close friends.

The party people made we wonder if I had lost the ability to understand complex social terms or at least figure out who was sleeping with whom. After two or three of these get togethers, I decided to live like a monk in this tundra town. Then, I fell in love.

Toward the end of winter, I met Susan and her boss on the steps of the Alaska Commercial Company store. Her supervisor said that they were both state social workers. Susan was wearing a blue down parka. Its heavy hood hid her hair and ears. But, it kept a cold breeze from stinging her face. She could have been missing one or both of her ears, something I decided in seconds that I could accept. I wouldn't confirm that she had two beautiful ears until next summer, when a strong breeze blew back her thick black locks.

A few weeks later, Susan would appear at one of my adoption hearings. The judge mispronounced her last name. I found the judge's mistake puzzling and her reaction charming. Would she want me to give up my celibacy vow or at least ask her out on a date?

After working up the courage, I invited Susan to dinner at my cabin the following Saturday. She surprised me by saying, "Yes."

I spent Saturday on my hands and knees cleaning the cabin's linoleum floor. All winter sooty smoke from my oil-fired range had darkened it. It took many hours to wash

A nice bottle of 1972 Pinot Noir

the grey away. Towards the end of the afternoon, I was worried that I would empty my 50-gallon water barrel before finishing the job.

A half hour before Susan was scheduled to arrive, I uncorked a bottle of California Pinot Noir that I had been saving for my first romantic Bethel dinner. She showed up on cross-country skis, which she had used to get from her roommate's house in the government subdivision to my cabin.

Earlier in the week, a powerful blizzard had covered the tundra with a thick layer of snow. In the Sierra Nevada Mountains, heavy winter storms like that would blanket everywhere with many feet of soft snow. In western towns like Bethel, high winds carried storm snow hundreds of miles across the tundra. It slammed into village buildings, like my little rental shack in Bethel, blocking the entry way with thick drifts. But enough had settled on the ground to let snowmachines drive just about anywhere. Susan used a series of snowgo tracks to ski over to my place.

Like most Bethel residents, Susan walked into my entryway and opened the front door without knocking. Then she said hello. The sound of her kicking snow off her ski boots tipped me to her presence.

After she entered my little two-roomed cabin, I hung up her parka on a wall peg while she took off her boots. I was glad that I had washed the floor or I would have had to tell her to keep her boots on so her socks wouldn't stain the insides of her boots when she put them back on.

I poured her a glass of wine, from which she took a polite sip and then set on my little kitchen table. While we ate, she told me that she didn't drink wine or beer. Even though I had saved the pinot all winter in hopes that it would impress a woman, I found Susan's rejection of it charming. Everything she said or did seemed charming. This is probably why I have little memory of what I cooked for dinner or the things that we talked about during the meal. I do remember being relieved when she invited me to go skiing with her after we ate.

Before that week, skiing involved a lot of slips and slides. A winter worth of wind had turned the earlier snow into concrete. But that night, our old wooden skis slid over the snow machine trails without effort. In what seem like minutes, we crossed Bethel town to a river bluff. There, we watched the light of a downriver snowmachine drive past.

Somewhere in my brain, I thought it was time to kiss Susan or at least give her a hug. But I remained frozen in place, keeping a socially acceptable distance from this woman with whom I was obsessed.

I don't remember much about returning to my cabin, where Susan invited me to ski again the next morning. This was Saturday night, when most folks my age stayed up late, slept in Sunday morning, and then headed over to the Kuskokwin Inn for burgers and fries. But I snapped out "great" when Susan said she would be back at my cabin mid-morning for a ski.

Eventuality, I fell asleep after listening to the public radio station shutdown. The DJ said goodnight then played two songs. The first was called "Tundra Shack" by a Kipnuk singer named Joe Jim Paul. The song ended with "biawaa," the Yupik slang word for goodbye.

No clouds blocked the blue sky when Susan showed up the next morning at my cabin. She stood in her skis while I clipped on mine and followed her across Brown Slough. We took a snowgo trail over a series of tundra bogs and through broad willow thickets, ending up at the place where two old paddle wheelers rotted quietly on the shore of Steamboat Slough.

Morning light brightened the snow and the bleached wooden planks of the boats. I thought about asking Susan to help me find a way of climbing onto the deck of the nearest steamboat. Then I worried about her getting hurt if we tried. Then I wondered what was happening to me. This was 1977. Women had already established the right for equal treatment as men in all things. But I was slipping back into 1950s America, where men were expected to sacrifice time and muscle to protect loved, fragile women from harm.

Crap.

Instead of losing cultural face, I asked Susan if she was ready to ski home. I'd like to say that I was emotionally back in the 1970s by the time we reached my cabin. But...

After Susan left that afternoon, I struggled to think of a way to build a romantic relationship for us or at least figure out how to hold her hand. Trying to kiss her might have chased her away. Hand holding was the best I could hope for.

The week before, Robert, another VISTA at Alaska Legal Services and I had made plans to dig out a snow cave on some bluffs near the Akiachak Trail, then use it for a campout. If he agreed, I'd invite Susan. All three of us could spend next Saturday night in our own sleeping bags. I'd arm wrestle with Robert if necessary to keep my sleeping bag between his and Susan's.

It took me a few days to work up the courage to ask Susan if she wanted to campout with us. It took her less than a second to say yes. Saturday morning, Susan, Robert and I walked a few miles along the Akiachak Trail looking for a snow-filled draw where we could dig out our cave. We flushed a covey of mating ptarmigan as we walked. Most of them flew off a few hundred feet. Some of the bright white birds froze in place. They were exposing themselves as easy targets for anyone with a rifle. It was mating season. Maybe the exposed ones that survived would have better luck with the hens.

Robert spotted the perfect place for digging our cave soon after we flushed the ptarmigan. There, a big chunk of blizzard snow half-filled a small creek bed. We grabbed our shovels and in a few minutes had dug out a hole large enough to form a cave opening. Then, we shoveled upwards until we established a rising channel. From there, Robert and Susan started digging out a room large enough for three sleeping bags.

As they expanded the snow cave. I took a spot just outside the door to keep the cave opening from being blocked by their shoveled snow. As my head rose and fell like a ptarmigan's while I moved snow from the cave opening, someone fired a bullet at my head. It was followed by several more bullets, each buzzing closer to my left ear than the one before. I pulled off my ptarmigan-colored wool cap from my head and tossed it in the air.

Then I shouted that I was not a ptarmigan. The shooter tucked his rifle into its scabbard and drove off on a snowgo that lacked an engine cover.

After a near death experience like mine, a smart, responsible person would have abandoned the snow shelter, walked back to town, and reported the shooting to the police. But Robert and Susan had been safe inside the expanding snow cave during the shooting. I was the target but refused to do anything that might discourage Susan from spending the night in the snow cave. We kept digging. But I did switch out my white wool cap for a Kelly green and gold Oakland A's cap. In another hour, we had what we needed.

Recently, I asked Susan what she remembered about our night in the snow cave. She gave me a hard look and pointed out that by forcing Robert and her to sleep on either side of me, I had made sure they would both be cold until dawn. I had to unzip my sleeping bag halfway through the night because sleeping between the two of them made me overheat.

Just a Ferryman

People in his village named their children after saints, so I will give him a holy pseudonym—"Augustine." His friends would call him "Auggie" or use the Yup'ik teasing name that his cousins gave him. He found destructive anger in bootleg whisky bottles like other decent men I met while working as a lawyer at a legal aid office in Bethel. Auggie was married to Elizabeth, somehow beautiful in spite of years of drunken beatings.

Auggie was passed out drunk when I first met Elizabeth. It was three in the afternoon on a summer Friday, only ninety minutes before the court closed for the weekend. Mary, the office paralegal and Yup'ik translator, greeted Elizabeth at the door with a sedate Yup'ik hello—"Cama-i."

"Iitu," Mary yelled in the direction of my bare plywood office. "Come, Big Eyes." She had given me that Yup'ik nickname a year ago, right after I had moved to Bethel. While I dug out a pen and legal pad from the mess on my desk, Mary asked Elizabeth to sit on our dusty couch and then filled a kettle with water dipped from a 50-gallon drum. It was warming on a hot plate when I took a seat across from Elizabeth. Even before she spoke, I knew that she needed a court order to keep her safe. Deep purple bruises spread across her apple cheeks and circled one of her dark brown eyes. Swollen flesh had closed over the other one.

Elizabeth and I sat in silence while Mary plopped tea bags into three mugs and filled them with boiling water. Mary delivered the darkening tea, took a seat on the couch, and waited with me for Elizabeth to speak.

In the Lower Forty-eight, I would have started with a question but that constituted rudeness in this Yup'ik place. Hard at any time, keeping the expected silence of respect with a little more than an hour before the court closed was almost impossible.

Five years after I met Elizabeth, a victim of domestic violence would be able to obtain a protective order by appearing at an informal court hearing. She wouldn't even need a lawyer. But that afternoon, Alaskan courts could only grant the order Elizabeth needed if she also filed for divorce. The time to draft and file a divorce complaint and a motion for a temporary restraining order ticked away as Elizabeth sipped her tea. She looked down at the chipped linoleum floor and whispered in Yup'ik, "Auggie scares me."

Mary translated for me and then told Elizabeth in Yup'ik and English, "We could get you a paper from court to help but you would have to leave Auggie, at least for a little bit."

Several minutes later Elizabeth said in English, "He catches fish and last fall brought home a moose."

Mary said, "You could get welfare and food stamps, at least for a little bit."

After another five minutes Elizabeth said, "He loves me when he's sober, nice when there are no bootleggers."

State law made bars and liquor stores illegal in Bethel but people could still legally drink. Those who traveled to Anchorage brought booze back as luggage. Big liquor stores in Anchorage made a nice profit on orders phoned in from Bethel by those without money to travel. Their customers swamped the Bethel airport Friday nights to pick up ordered alcohol. Most carried away twin cases of beer that had been duct-taped together by the liquor store. Bootleggers grabbed cardboard boxes full of hard liquor. People drank their own beer but bootleggers resold much of their whiskey for four times what they paid for it. When he had forty dollars and enough wild-caught food put by for the kids, Auggie bought bootlegged Canadian whiskey.

I never drank bootlegged booze but did make many trips by cab out to the airport to pick up duct-taped beer. My tendency to fall asleep halfway through my second can of brew kept it a recreational drug. Alcohol's ability to draw violence from normally kind people, Native or not, tore up many families on the Kuskokwim River. Only a lawyer, I couldn't stop the pain, just seek legal protection for the victim or defend in court the one who did the damage. I didn't wield *Excalibur* or lift Diogenes' lantern, only navigated clients through their court proceedings. I was Elizabeth's legal boatman, not her guardian.

✳

Elizabeth sat without speaking for five minutes before she finally asked for help and gave me the information I needed for the court paperwork. I called the courthouse and warned the judge that I would be over to file for Elizabeth's restraining order. He agreed to stay late. At a quarter to five, he signed a temporary restraining order (TRO) that would make Auggie a criminal if he approached Elizabeth during the next ten days. With the help of a BIA social worker who was willing to bend the general assistance rules, Elizabeth checked into the Kusko Inn under a fake name. Her kids stayed with her sister. She had enough credit from the BIA for several days of meals at the hotel restaurant. Mary brought her a copy of the TRO and a number to call the police dispatcher if Auggie came around. She also dropped off a copy of the order at the police station.

Back at the office, Mary, the eyes in her broad, round face half-closed in a smile, wished me a good weekend, as she had the previous Friday, when the most exciting event was the weekly visit of the man who emptied the bucket of human waste from the office restroom. Mary showed no fear of Auggie, even though she had kids at home and everyone knew that she worked in our office. I followed Mary's lead and tried not to think about Auggie and Elizabeth until Monday.

Elizabeth spent the weekend marooned in a hotel room with dark-paneled walls too thin to block out the sounds of lovemaking in the adjacent rooms. Unlike her house, she had cable TV, no kids to distract her, and running water. She had a mirror in which she could study her damaged face.

On Monday, Mary saw Auggie walk up to the office and told me to meet him at the door. He smelled like old salmon scales and drinker's sweat but appeared sober. I asked him to come have tea in the waiting room. He followed me, the TRO clutched in his right fist, then took a seat on the couch. As I filled the kettle with dip water, he shouted, "Give her back." When I turned to face him, he tore up the TRO. "Give her back," he shouted again as shreds of the order drifted to the dusty floor.

I was scared even though Auggie had no gun, no weapon of any kind, just his fists. I had been working in the office for two years but had never been around someone so angry unless they were drunk. Auggie was sober. His eyes watered as he broke off eye contact to study his hands. "Give her back," he whispered, and then headed to the office door. Rather than relief that Auggie had left without hitting me, I felt guilty for causing him pain.

❋

After arguing my first case before the Alaska Supreme Court, I had stopped assuming that my legal work always benefited the families of my clients. During oral argument, one of the justices had asked if I really expected them to reverse, on a technicality, the order terminating the parental rights of my client. She had beaten her two-year-old child with a belt and burned him with a cigarette. The question did not stop me from arguing another technical appeal point. That night, after the adrenaline rush had played out, I let myself wonder, for the first time, what I had done. If my clients lost, a loving family would adopt the child. If I won, the kid might live for years in a series of foster homes. I had honored the lawyer's code of ethics and zealously represented my client, had taken every permissible step to get her what she wanted. I did not fall asleep that night until I accepted the limitations of my power and responsibility. Without concern for any interest but hers, I had delivered my client's best arguments to the court and guided her through court proceedings. We both had to wait on the riverbank for the court to decide whether she had lost her child. I passed the responsibility onto the legal system, the justices, and the lawyer who had argued the state's case. If I won, the fault belonged to one who violated my client's trial rights or failed to adequately present the state's case.

The night after Auggie's office visit, I stopped feeling guilty. He was the one who drank the booze, then beat the woman he loved. I passed him the responsibility for the court order that had divided his family.

Elizabeth called on Thursday and said, "He loves me and won't hit me again."

I asked, "Are you home with him?

"Ii-i, yes."

"Are you going to stay with him?"

"Yes."

"I'll tell the judge."

The next time Elizabeth asked for help, it took less time to write up a complaint and motion for a restraining order. I already had all the information I needed. It was harder to convince the social worker to pick up the tab for Elizabeth's stay at the local hotel and to talk the judge into signing the TRO.

Two days after the judge signed the order, Elizabeth called to tell me, "Auggie loves me."

The third time she came to the office, two blackened eyes convinced me to again protect Elizabeth from her husband.

Ignorant of what compelled Elizabeth to return to her cycle of violence, I vowed not to get her another protective order if she let Auggie back into her house. But the fear that showed in her eyes during a fourth office visit convinced me to seek another one.

I didn't hear from either Elizabeth or Auggie again. Mary told me that they had moved to Anchorage.

Whether to live the kind of happy life that people enjoy in TV shows or to escape sadness and violence at home, many young people moved from the river to Anchorage. They settled in neighborhoods already home to earlier immigrants from Western Alaska. Since the ability to kill or skin a seal meant little in Anchorage, many returned home or joined the

Anchorage homeless. Auggie and Elizabeth simply disappeared into the state's largest village.

My client for the Alaska Supreme Court appeal may have lived in Anchorage while she waited to learn whether she would get back her then six-year-old son. It took four and a half years of trial court hearings and appeals before she would know. While she waited, the child learned language and love from a man and a woman he called "Dad" and "Mom." I can only imagine the pain the boy and people he believed to be his parents would have felt if the court returned him to my client. But I never let those products of my imagination discourage me from doing my best for my clients or the other parents that I represented in termination trials. For almost forty years, I followed the lawyer's Rules of Professional Responsibility and worked hard within the law, to satisfy my clients. It didn't matter if they wore a Yup'ik kuspuk, prison orange, or the business casual attire of a state worker.

Other battered women sought help during my five years of service in the legal aid office. Their cases generally followed the pattern set by Elizabeth. A white woman new to Bethel, Martha Smith, walked in the door with an unblemished face. She looked out the window or at the office door as I conducted a Lower 48-style client interview.

"Did he assault you?"

"He hit me where no one could see the bruises."

"Please point to where he struck you."

After touching her breasts, genitals, stomach, and the patch of skin over her kidneys, she said, "Once, he slowly loaded bullets into the cylinder of his gun, pulled back the hammer and said he'd shoot me if I didn't apologize for talking back."

"What did you do?"

"I told him what he wanted to hear."

"Why did you leave him?"

Before she could answer I said, "I mean, how did you leave him?"

"One day, when he was visiting his mother in Billings, I packed up some clothes, cleaned out our bank account, and flew to Anchorage."

"How did you end up in Bethel?

"Somebody in Anchorage told me they were looking for waitresses at the Kuskokwim Inn."

"How did he find you?"

"I don't know. One night, during the dinner shift, I found him sitting at a table. He followed me home. I just opened the door of my place and let him in."

Martha asked for help on a Monday morning and we were in court two days later. Her husband sat in the back of an otherwise empty courtroom while Martha and I sat at counsel table. I experienced some of the fear that Martha had felt every day since she had married the tall, hard man. From what she told me, her husband had come to Bethel to regain control of his wife, not to seek her forgiveness. As the black-robed judge entered the courtroom, I wondered if Martha would again yield to her bully.

The judge had to ask Martha to speak up several times during her testimony. She looked away from her husband when she described his fists striking her breasts, privates, back, and stomach and how he pointed the revolver at her. The husband leaped up and shouted, "Judge, she is lying. Martha, if you don't stop lying, I am going to teach you the value of truth." The judge told him to sit down until it was his turn to testify. I was encouraged by the look the judge gave him because it was the one he'd given me just before denying a recent motion. When Martha answered my final question, the judge asked her husband if he wanted to cross-examine. He stood up, nodded yes, then said to Martha, "Tell the judge what this is really about."

"I don't know what you mean."

"You go out of your way to piss me off. Sometimes, you hit me first."

"Objection, Judge, he is testifying, not asking a question."

"Sustained, Mr. Branch."

The judge told Martha that she did not have to respond to her husband's demand. She blushed and started to speak until I shook my head. Her husband didn't testify after Martha left the witness stand. The judge told us he would sign the order without asking me for a closing argument.

Martha took refuge in an empty courtroom while her husband and I waited for the clerk to make copies of the restraining order. I could see the police station out the window and wondered how much damage he could do to me before someone responded to a 911 call from the clerk. He broke while he read his copy of the order. Martha left the courtroom and walked up to her sobbing husband. He raised his face, blotched and snotty, to look at her.

"I am sorry, Martha. Let me take you home."

She had forgiven him before when he cried and said he was sorry. I expected her to comfort him to silence and ask me to get the order vacated. Then she would have been like all the clients who had returned to danger for love. I would have had no choice but to pass on her request for the court to vacate the hard-won order. That's the lawyer's charter—do the client's bidding, even when honoring a self-destructive request. But she left her sobbing batterer, protective order in hand. I couldn't pump my fist or even claim victory. I was only Martha's ferryman, fighting legal currents to carry her to her chosen destination.

Because I Asked

Kuskokwim 300 starting chute, January 18, 1984, noon. Full sun, clear, little wind, moderate temperatures (ten to twenty-five degrees).

On snow stained with urine and dog scat, my team strained against their harnesses and jerked the sled. I couldn't hear the public address announcer over the sound of the other dog teams. Without being asked, the collie-like Bilbo led my dogs into the starting chute of the 1984 Kuskokwim 300: one of the mid-distance dog races that qualify mushers for the more famous and longer Iditarod Race.

    With only eleven dogs, mine was one of the smaller teams. Two mushers were already on the race trail that led up the Kuskokwim to the halfway point at Aniak. The trail then looped east to the checker's wall tent at Whitefish Lake and returned to the Kuskokwim. From there, mushers who had not scratched would return downriver to Bethel. A soccer mom's minivan could cover the same distance in five hours. The year before I ran the Kusko, the winner finished in just under sixty-six. The final musher crossed the line thirty hours later.

    Behind us, thirty-four teams of tightly wound, well-conditioned dogs waited impatiently for their starting time slot. Most would finish before my team. I lacked the drive to push the dogs hard enough to win or even be competitive. The race was just a chance to prove that Bilbo and the dogs he led were a tough, honest team that could complete the route.

Because I asked, Bilbo worked when tired or bored. During training runs, he could drag the team into forty-mile-an-hour winds that drove the wind chill to eighty below zero. After I gave the go command, I could turn my back to the wind or pull a fur parka ruff over my numb face to keep it from freezing. The wind must have stung Bilbo when it collapsed the dense fur on his face but he'd never hesitated.

The white, wolf-like Neva usually ran in front next to Bilbo. She lacked his brains and loyalty but could trot at the head of the team for hours. Hooter, a blue-eyed, brindled husky, was paired with the sweet-tempered, flopped-eared O.J. Driven by the great hunger bred into Alaska sled dogs, Hooter once survived eating his dog harness. Behind them ran two loaners—Whitey, a 14-year-old lead dog from the team of a Bethel Yup'ik elder, and Pepper, a high-strung beagle mix. Just in front of the sled ran a crafty, often-feisty dog named Trotski, my penance for some terrible sin. With a thick orange and white coat, he looked like a surly teddy bear.

While a race official counted down the seconds to our start time, my team ramped up their efforts to break free. I considered letting the excited Bilbo set the pace. But I couldn't afford to waste the dogs' energy. The odds of a rookie like me being able to finish were already poor. Over a third of the teams had scratched during the previous year's race.

The Kusko had a well-earned reputation for bad weather and difficult conditions. Low temperatures and high winds drove the wind chill down to one hundred below zero during the first thirty-six hours of the 1980 inaugural race. On the homebound leg the temperature skyrocketed to forty degrees and rain fell, giving the snow the consistency of cooked oatmeal. My dogs were used to low wind chills but a struggle in thick, bottomless snow would have broken them.

Bethel to Tuluksak. Fifty-three miles. Traveled noon to 10:00 p.m., full sun, clear, moderate temperatures (ten to twenty-five degrees).

The competitive teams passed us before we reached the first checkpoint at Akiachak. None of their drivers smiled. Susan Butcher, who would later gain national attention for her four Iditarod race wins, eyed Trotski as he tried to pull our sled into her path. She then watched Bilbo for a sign

Dan drives the Kusko 300 dog team to the
starting line, *January, 1985*

that he could control his team. Apparently willing to trust my leader, she
called out, "On by." Hearing this order to pass, Butcher's leader swung
her team around us as I slowed mine with the sled brake. I don't know if
it was Granite that led her past Trotski. That husky would lead Butcher's
teams to three Iditarod victories and in 1988 receive the Golden Harness
for being the best lead dog in the race.

Like Bilbo, Granite must have pulled Susan's team away from open
water and dog fights. He led them over the glare ice of Norton Sound while
a north wind slammed crystallized snow into his face. Did Susan enjoy
the same satisfaction that I received each time Bilbo pulled the team right
when I said "gee" or left when he heard "haw." Like me, she must have
seen her lead dog as partner and friend, not pet or farm animal.

Only multiple Iditarod winner Rick Swenson spoke to me as he passed
erect on his sled runners. A hi-tech, insulated hat covered all but the bill
of his ball cap. His earflaps lifted up when he turned into the wind to ask
me, "Did you buy that little flop-eared brown and black one from me?"

I hadn't, but he was a shrinking figure in insulated overalls before I could tell him. So ended my brief brush with mushing royalty.

Swenson passed me just before the trail dropped onto the Kuskokwim River from a tundra bluff. We had to cross a strip of overflow water that had flooded onto the ice at high tide. I trusted Bilbo to lead us through it to dry trail. More than once he had pulled the team and me out of the water when we broke through thin ice. He didn't hesitate to trot through the knee-deep overflow. I only had to ask. The other dogs followed. I kept my feet dry by pivoting headfirst over the sled handlebar.

We left the Kuskokwim for the narrower Qweek River and then crossed through the frozen-swamp forest of black spruce and willow that abuts the Yup'ik village of Akiachak. From the trail, the spindly conifers looked like a thick forest, but I knew they were just a loose scattering of ancient, slow-growing trees on a marshy plain.

Like the other mushers, I stopped at the Akiachak checkpoint just long enough to sign in with the checker and find the line of fluorescent-orange-tipped wooden stakes that marked the way out of town. Squeezed onto a low bluff dominated by an unlit airstrip, the villagers lived in boxy plywood houses. All had snowmachines or dogsleds parked near wooden pole racks hung with fishnets and drying pike.

Late afternoon light bounced off a crescent of open water between the trail and the river's shore near Akiak. A Bethel musher training for the race had fallen through it the previous month. No one found his body. The bright water reminded me of the beautiful widow he left behind, and their confused child. I lived then with an independent woman who would eventually agree to marry me. Our daughter wouldn't arrive for five more years. Her birth brought caution with responsibility. But the year I ran the 300, I retained the arrogance of a teenaged boy. I never considered that the open water, or any other race hazard, could threaten my life.

I pulled over for a four-hour break just downriver from Tuluksak so the dogs could rest away from the distractions of the village. Like most of the country drained by the Kuskokwim, almost all as flat as lake ice, the place offered little view. But, in that late afternoon sunlight, the Kuskokwim

River displayed a snow queen beauty that ended on the far shore where bare willows formed a low, dark horizon.

A few of the tail-end teams passed as my dogs chomped down a high-fat-and-protein kibble mixed with water that I had carried from Bethel in a beer cooler. Light from a full moon made it easier to collect the dog's empty food bowls and check their feet for cuts or tenderness. After packing everything away in the sled bag, I stretched out but couldn't sleep. I was warm enough in my insulated coveralls, beaver hat, and white, pneumatic bunny boots but too excited to drop off. As the dogs slept, I watched the moon. Later, a curtain of pale green then red northern lights rippled across the sky.

At 10:00 p.m., I clipped the dogs to the gangline and let Bilbo led us to the Tuluksak checkpoint. Acting as happy as I felt, they loped into the village. It took three men to hold them while a race official checked that my sled bag contained the required sleeping bag, axe, food, and warm clothes. I wanted to leave right away and let the dogs burn up their energy on the trail but a high school kid approached and asked me to sign a Kusko 300 calendar.

During the previous year's race, mushers had taken extended breaks in the village. Before my race, the high school held a lottery to choose which student would be able to help each musher. This year, most teams pushed through toward the next checkpoint without even meeting their assigned helpers. I wanted to do the same but the young man treated me with an undeserved deference, as if I were an NBA star. Honored, and at the same time feeling guilty for making him wait while my dogs rested just outside the village, I anchored the team and went with him for water.

Returning with a sloshing bucket and my only fan, I found Whitey, my fourteen-year-old backup leader, limping. A little blood seeped from a leg wound inflicted by Trotski. That furry thug had mugged the toothless old dog for a scrap of food he had dug out of the snow. I thanked God that Bilbo was OK. A race veterinarian told me that Whitey would recover from his injuries, but not until after the race. I left him with the dropped-dog handler. The village checker told me we were dead last.

Tuluksak to Lower Kalskag: Forty-five miles. Traveled 11:00 p.m. to 11:00 a.m., clear, little wind, moderate temperatures (minus ten to zero degrees).

Bilbo pulled us onto a Tuluksak River trail that led to the next checkpoint at Lower Kalskag. The dogs trotted up the river and entered a series of connected back sloughs. Northern lights floated over the well-packed trails. Euphoria replaced my post dogfight depression. I forgot that in the wild, mood swings can signal danger. Irrational joy can lead to irrational choices.

We passed a small meadow lit by a pyramid-shaped fire. Three men stood near it. Their bodies threw dramatic shadows on the snow like figures in a Caravaggio painting. At the meadow's edge, canine eyes burned red in the light of my headlamp beam. Seconds later we returned to darkness.

I took out my Walkman and turned it on. Rather than the first notes of Beethoven's "Sixth Symphony" that I had expected, I heard Michael Jackson's "Thriller." Jackson sang of being touched by cold hands in the darkness as the dogs suddenly bunched up. While I looked for a crack into which I could jam the welded steel sled anchor, Jackson urged me to close my eyes and ignore danger. I kicked the anchor into a crack and ran to Bilbo. The high tenor warned that I would fight for my life in the black night as Hooter's teammates growled and searched for dog snacks left behind by another dog musher. Before I could grab Bilbo and straighten out the team by pulling him free of the tangle, Trotski crunched on Singer's leg. All the other dogs turned on Singer. Between warning growls and sharp-edged barks, the gentle dogs tore at each other. I worked with bare hands to stop the biting while Vincent Price recited Jackson's poem about death in the darkness.

Trotski survived without a scratch. None of the others were bleeding badly but Singer and another dog limped and winced when I touched the dense muscles of their upper legs. They all would recover from their wounds but some might have to drop out of the race. My glasses broke during the melee and I didn't have a backup pair. Until I replaced them, I'd have a hard time seeing down the trail more than a couple of dog team lengths.

It was 3:00 a.m., the witching hour. Alone, vision impaired, softened by lack of sleep, depression settled over me. If I lost three more dogs, my race would be over.

With a Coleman camp stove battered by many sled rides, I heated water and kibble for the dogs. After they ate, I stretched out on the sled bag. Three dog teams, maybe those I saw in the romantically lit meadow, passed our makeshift camp. At 7:00 a.m., I packed and headed up the trail to Lower Kalskag. Singer rode inside the sled. The other fight victims resisted my attempts to drop them into the sled bag so I hitched them to the gangline.

The guys slowed often to snatch bits of snacks dropped by other mushers. Rather than scold, which would have further dampened their spirits and mine, I tried different lead dogs. After each of my most promising candidates failed, I clipped in Hooter—a dog short on brains but long on stamina. He dragged the whole team up the trail.

Slack formed in the normally honest Pepper's tug line. Still trying to please, K.C. kept his ears erect but after a few hours he let his tug line flop. When we moved onto the Kuskokwim River, twelve-inch-high streams of fine snow blew across the trail. Just before dawn at 10:00 a.m., I stopped for one of our hourly snack breaks, tossing each dog a chunk of raw, frozen silver salmon. Encouraged by the way they wolfed down the fish, I allowed myself a little hope. Singer stuck his nose out of the sled bag and grabbed a piece of fish out of my hand. *You little faker*, I thought.

The rising sun revealed empty fish camps downriver from Lower Kalskag. My guys picked up the pace as if their spirits climbed with the sun.

Mine did. I found beauty in the simple geometry of diminutive fish camp shelters, the rectangle smokehouses, and spruce-wood fish racks secured at right angles to five-foot-high posts. "We can make it, guys," I told the team and then I muttered it to myself. A mile farther up the trail Pepper dropped to the ground, followed by K.C. Both joined Singer in the canvas sled bag. They couldn't curl up in the gear-choked bag so they rode with snouts pointed forward and used their front legs to keep from sliding. The other dogs still pulled. I ran behind the sled to lighten their load. If the loss of three of the team didn't break my dogs, I wouldn't let it break me.

In Lower Kalskag, I secured the sled and went inside the checkpoint building. A volunteer doctor from Bethel jammed a glass of water into my hand and told me I was dehydrated. I longed for coffee. My eyes slowly focused on a soap opera flickering on the screen of a tiny black and white TV.

Lower Kalskag to Upper Kalskag. Nine miles, traveled 12:00 a.m. to 1:00 p.m., full sun, clear, little wind, moderate temperature (10 degrees).

I went outside, stepped on the sled, and hollered, "Hike." Bilbo and Hooter jumped up and led the team on the short run to Upper Kalskag. When two ravens flew over us, the dogs broke into a lope. The sled banged over the bumpy trail, giving the wounded a short but rough ride into Upper. I was surprised to see teams of scratched mushers. After my apocalyptic night, I had assumed that I'd bagged all the bad race luck.

A race veterinarian looked over the three dogs in the sled basket. Both Pepper and K.C. had pulled muscles that knocked them out of the race but he cleared Singer. The wheel dog first limped on his right side and then placed his whole weight on it trying to affect a limp on his left. He got a shot of vitamins and was returned to the team.

I walked over to the race cache and dug out a burlap sack of dog food that I had dropped off at the Bethel airport before the race. I poured enough for one meal into my big cook pot, added water from the village school, and filled eight dog bowls with the resulting gruel. They sucked it down before it could freeze solid. I breakfasted on fresh oranges, eggs, and fry bread at the community hall, then used the village's one phone to arrange for someone to send my old black horn-rimmed glasses to Aniak. They'd make me look like a bearded Buddy Holly, but at least I would be able to see my competition pull away.

While my dogs rested, Rick Swenson blew through Upper Kalskag on his way back to Bethel. He had already completed the seventy-mile loop through Aniak and the halfway point at Whitefish Lake.

The race marshal, Dick Mackey, watched Swenson head downriver for Bethel. Six years earlier, my Pepper had helped Mackey beat Swenson in the Iditarod. Pepper was already in the dropped dog lot and Mr. Mackey didn't know how hard I'd trained. I was just a guy in trouble at the back of the pack. When Mackey's compact body blocked my sun, I looked up from my sled bag and saw a kind, mustachioed face with the eyes of a man about to deliver bad news. He must have heard about my dropped dogs and slow progress—things he would expect from a rookie musher who hadn't properly conditioned his team. Just before he ordered me to scratch, Mackey grabbed my sled handle with his right hand. Bilbo and the guys hopped up, ready for the run to Aniak.

He said, "Huh? These dogs are in good shape. What are you hauling in this sled?"

"Just what I need to camp out—survival tent, sleeping pad and bag, camp stove, gas, cook pot and bowls, frozen salmon for dog snacks, dried salmon for me, axe, emergency medical kit, steel tie out cable for the dogs, one thousand cloth dog booties, and adhesive tape."

Looking back at the now-eager dogs, he said, "I guess you can stay in the race unless you fall too far behind but you should get rid of some of that junk. This is a race, not a trapline run."

Upper Kalskag to Aniak. Twenty-six miles. Traveled late afternoon to evening. Clear, wind gusts from gaps in mountains on west side of river, blinding, blowing snow, moderate temperatures (minus five degrees), minus zero wind chill.

All my dropped dogs were loaners from other mushers. I left the village with the family—eight dogs that I had run for several years before the race. A bond of loyalty had built up after countless feedings, caresses, and training miles. Would that bond hold until we reached the finish line?

From Upper Kalskag, we continued up the Kuskokwim River, now bordered on one side by spruce-covered hills. In exposed sections wind-driven snow blinded me. Bilbo had brought me home through more than one blizzard, so I let him choose the trail.

In Aniak, I had to search half-an-hour for the checker. He had gone home because he thought we wouldn't arrive for several more hours. He handed me the pair of black horn-rimmed glasses that a volunteer pilot had brought from Bethel.

"You can find food over at the Sackett Hall, down where all the snowgos are parked."

The generous people of the village of three hundred had set out a large buffet—a diversity of dishes reflecting the cultural mix of this old mining town. Yup'ik and Athabaskan foods sat beside Lower-48 style hot dishes, pasta, and sheet cakes. I passed on the tuna casserole cooked with cream of mushroom soup by a schoolteacher from Minnesota and wolfed down rice, caribou, and moose.

After a friend promised to wake me in five hours, I showered, brushed my teeth, and slept. Waking, I pulled on wool pants and a shirt that smelled like flop sweat, and climbed into my green Walls insulated overalls. The dogs, acting fit after nine hours' rest, looked ready to finish the race. I was in last place but my team still loped out of the village.

Aniak to wall tent checkpoint at Whitefish Lake. Thirty-seven miles. Traveled sunrise to early afternoon, full sun, clear, little wind, colder temperatures (minus twenty degrees).

After an initial gallop, the dogs trotted onto a mine access trail cut by a Caterpillar through white spruce forest. In an hour we left the trees and crossed a tundra lake scoured clean of snow except for a strip packed down by snowmachines. The trail pointed at Hamilton and other round-shouldered Kuskokwim Mountains. In the foreground, the flashing yellow light of a traffic barricade marked a turn that many of the prior year's racers had missed. Seeing this icon of New York reminded me that I was in a race, not on a camping trip. I could have ignored the message. Those tracking race progress in Bethel had already named me "Camp Along Dan."

In later years, the race would discourage untested mushers like me. But that year a hobbyist could still race the great ones. I had a chance to travel through country too remote for me to reach without food drops.

Bilbo's team moved with pace along a trail that crossed small lakes and in and out of narrow streambeds. The temperature dropped, which made my plastic sled runners squeak and drag, rather than slip over the snow. To stay warm, I ran behind the sled.

At the checkpoint, I directed the dogs off the lake and into a shallow bowl surrounded by a wall of white spruce and birch trees. The checker had already packed his sled. Before driving off, he told me that Rick Swenson had won the race and that it was twenty below zero.

I staked out the dogs and used the checker's campfire to melt snow and cook up a hot meal for them. Bright sun reduced everything to primary

Dogs taking a snack break midway
through the Kusko 300 Sled Dog Race

colors–a child's blue sky, pure white snow, crayon green and brown trees. After eating, my dogs rested, protected from tundra wind by a low berm. Gone, for the moment, were my worries about the race, weather, and dropped dogs; gone like the Whitefish checker and the other mushers.

A wolf head rose above the berm followed by a dozen more. I tried to blink away the hallucination but the wolves wouldn't disappear. They cocked their white or gray or black heads, sniffed the air, and eyed the snow for food. Later, a pilot would tell me that the pack followed behind the last place musher to clean up any snacks abandoned by the race teams. My guys showed no interest in the wolves, and I was too blissed out to work up any fear, so I treated the wolf pack as an hallucination, and we all spent a quiet three hours at the checkpoint.

Whitefish Lake to Upper Kalskag. Twenty-one miles. Traveled late afternoon to evening, full sun, clear, little wind, colder temperature (minus twenty degrees).

We trotted down a winding stream then up a long grade forested with paper birch and white spruce. The sled slowed like a roller coaster on approach to the first drop off. Bilbo disappeared from sight where the trail plunged down a steep stream bank. Like teeth in a zipper, each pair of dogs clicked out of sight. I managed to hold on to the sled as it shot down the bank. The dogs all turned left when they reached the stream. The sled flipped on its side. Now stretched full out on the snow, I slid behind the tipped sled until the dogs stopped next to eleven green Absorbine Junior liniment bottles scattered on the slough ice. I righted the sled and made sure nothing had fallen out of the sled bag before saying "Hike." Bilbo pulled the team back onto the trail.

A mile down the trail we found an overweight white man from Bethel running Absorbine Junior into the shoulder of his wheel dog. I told him about Swenson's victory then said, "You'll be the new Red Lantern if I pass you." He smiled, walked to his sled bag, pulled out a quart bottle of Black Velvet whiskey, and said that he had just changed his race strategy.

The checker was nowhere to be found when we arrived in Upper Kalskag. At the checkpoint building, a Cup'ik musher from Chevak slept sprawled like a refugee on the floor. Two white mushers from his village sat with their backs against the wall. They stared into space like shell-shocked soldiers. Lacking the money to fly their outfits to Bethel, the men had used their dogs to pull them 150 miles over flat, windy tundra from their Bering Sea village to the starting line. Unless they finished in the money, they would have to return home the same way.

After feeding my dogs and checking their feet, I left the dogs to rest and escaped into old copies of *Reader's Digest* magazines at the checkpoint.

Upper Kalskag to Tuluksak. Fifty-four miles. Traveled midnight to pre-dawn, clear, little wind, cold (minus forty degrees).

We left the village alone, trotted past the log houses of Lower Kalskag, then dropped onto the Kuskokwim River for the run to Tuluksak. Twenty miles later, Bilbo slowed the pace. He looked back often as if seeking permission to dig in for the night. "Bilbo," I said, "do you think the Raiders have a shot at winning the Super Bowl on Sunday?" When he showed no interest in football, I ran through the likely roster for the Dodgers next April. He reduced speed further after I told my only joke—the one about the sadist and masochist. I thought about singing some joy into him but it was 3:00 a.m. and we were close to the scene of the big dogfight. I could only remember the words of "Ashes of Love" and "Dark as a Dungeon."

"Guys, I'm as tired as you act," I said. "Let's take a nap." Nothing broke the darkness except the weak beam of my headlamp. After setting the snow anchor I clicked off the light and stretched out on the sled bag, ready to add another chapter to the legend of "Camp Along Dan." Before I could drop off, the sled jerked as three teams pulled up—the Chevakers.

We cooperated on the trail. Like bike racers in le Tour de France, three of our four teams followed in the lee of the lead team until it slowed. Then, the other teams passed so the former leader could rest at the back of the pelaton. When it wasn't my turn to lead, I relaxed and warmed my numb nose and cheeks with a bare hand. This stopped frostbite but fogged up my Buddy Holly horn rims. In the subzero night, breath that rose through my fingers instantly frosted over the lens. I watched most of the race through an icy gauze.

While in front of the pelaton, my dogs bunched up, as they did just before the big fight on the first night of the race. I slammed on the brakes and peered at what looked like a wind-felled spruce. It turned out to be a sled without any dogs connected to it. A musher from Bethel sat upright in the sled, sharing a sleeping bag with a bleeding dog. Between shivering fits, she said that a fight had broken out while she had snacked her dogs. She tried to break it up by firing her pistol over their heads. After the fight ended, she unsnapped her dogs from the gangline and secured them to trailside willows. Even though it was forty below zero, her head and hands were bare. She was hypothermic and needed to reverse her drop in core temperature. Other than encouraging her to put on her hat and mittens, I didn't know how to help. The Chevak guys did and probably saved her life.

Simon, the Cup'ik seal hunter, dug out a battered Coleman two-burner from his sled bag. With only thin cotton gloves protecting his hands from the cold, he managed to fire up the stove. While I snacked my team, Simon melted snow and then added small chunks of seal meat to the pot to warm up the other musher. Simon and a Chevaker named Buck stayed to help while Ray joined me on the run into Tuluksak.

At sunrise on Saturday morning, Ray and I pulled into Tuluksak. I checked in and told the race officials about the troubled musher. The dogs came next. After feeding them, I checked their feet for cuts or soreness, then headed over to Joe Demantle's house for a breakfast of moose stew, chicken, and his wife's fresh-baked bread.

Tuluksak to Yup'ik village of Akiak. Twenty-five miles. Traveled sunset to mid-evening, full sun then clear night, cold (minus forty degrees.

Camp Along Dan let his dogs rest in Tuluksak too long. Two of the Chevakers and the now-recovered Bethel musher left for the finish line while we rested. I had expected the woman to scratch. But, as a testament to seal meat and her fortitude, she beat me to Bethel. Bilbo and the other dogs stiffened up during the long break and could not stand without my help. After I lifted each off the snow, they stumbled out of the village like participants in a Monty Python silly-walk contest. Worry for them prevented me from enjoying how the late afternoon light threw long shadows from the stiff dogs onto the snow. Ice fog rose like steam from their backs. The dogs' muscles loosened just before they left the Tuluksak River. They trotted comfortably onto the broader Kuskokwim.

Ray, the Chevaker who left Tuluksak with us, had dropped his last leader in the village. I agreed to help him make it to Bethel.

I barely noticed the passage of time on the run to Akiak. In the village a friend invited me to his son's birthday party. I should have pressed on. The dogs didn't need a rest and with thirty miles to go, I was only three to four hours' running time from the Bethel finish line. A competitor would have skipped the party but it is considered rude in Yup'ik culture to say "no," so Camp Along Dan accepted. Having no choice, Ray waited while I stumbled through the village to the party.

Akiak to Yup'ik village of Kwethluk. Traveled late evening to early morning, clear, little wind, cold (minus forty degrees).

The Akiak checker briefed me on the trail out of town. "You are really going to like it, not like before when the trail just went on the river and the Kuskokuak shortcut. You are really going to like it. But it's kind of steep where it goes on the Kuskokuak Slough." I did not like it.

The trail snaked in and out of tiny sloughs and streams. All had short but steep banks that took a lot out of the wheel dogs and me when we had to muscle the heavy sled up to their summits.

About two hours out of Akiak, we had to stop and wait for Ray. My dogs dug resting spots in the snow. When I yelled "hike" they stood stiffly but didn't move down the trail. Bilbo settled back into his nest. I ran forward and lifted him and the others to a standing position but they collapsed back on the snow before I could run back to the sled. On the third try, the dogs slow-walked toward the next checkpoint at Kwethluk. They picked up speed as we moved along the top of a rolling bluff then charged down forty feet of steep bank onto Kuskokuak Slough where the sled tipped over. *This*, I thought, *must be the kind of steep part that the Akiak checker mentioned.*

Earlier in the winter, a thick flat platform of ice had formed over the slough, unaffected by the air gap that opened beneath it at low tide. That night its center, made thick and heavy by the recent cold weather, collapsed. An artillery barrage of booms and groans sounded as the ice cratered onto the surface of the river. The sounds spooked the dogs. I was more shaken by a cartoon fire that raced through the trailside willows, something only I could see.

While my dogs snacked on frozen silver salmon, I gathered wood for a warming fire. Even next to the fire, it was too cold to get any rest on the slough. After a few hours, we broke camp. When I asked, Bilbo stood and led our team toward home.

We found the Kwethluk checker sitting by a folding card table set up in the middle of the Kwethluk River. It was seven on Sunday morning. Without speaking, he handed me the sign-in clipboard. I wanted to ask him if he had held a river vigil all night and how far we were behind. But I couldn't see his face in the dark and nothing about his posture encouraged conversation.

Kwethluk to Bethel finish line. Fourteen miles. Traveled early morning to after sunrise, clear, twenty miles per hour north wind, cold (minus forty degrees), significant wind chill.

Neva led us onto the Kuskokwim where Ray managed, with much verbal encouragement, to force his team past us. I stood on the brake to let him put some distance between our teams. We had fewer than fourteen miles left in the race. I cleaned my eyeglass lens of frost and watched the rising sun flood the river and tundra with a clarifying light.

One obstacle remained and I wasn't sure we could get around it. The race trail would take us down a snowmachine path we used to return home from training runs. We would have to turn off it 1.5 miles from our dog yard. After three hundred miles of travel, would Bilbo lead the team away from home?

We climbed off the river and onto to the tundra bluffs trail that linked Akiachak with Bethel. A north wind gained strength at my back. Feeling warmth from the rising sun on my face, I fell asleep on the sled runners about seven miles from the finish line and four from the dreaded trail junction. Without being asked, Bilbo led the team away from home to the finish line. I woke up one hundred yards from the end. Someone I didn't recognize ran up and hugged me, then handed me a beer can. During the night, a half-inch thick barrier of frozen breath had formed on my mustache. While I tried to thaw it with a bare hand so I could drink the beer, I recognized the stranger as my father and the woman standing next to him as my partner, Susan.

Bethel. Race end. Clear, sixty below wind chill.

We didn't win the red lantern. Something stirred the Black Velvet drinker to finish and steal the honor. I still have the bronze belt buckle awarded to all the finishers. The dogs got nothing after the race but a long rest.

During the ninety-five hours it took us to finish, the affection that I felt for Bilbo and his team before the race deepened into love. They had kept moving when bored or in pain because I had asked.

'57 Chevy

I loaded two Evinrude six-gallon gas tanks into the back of my 1957 Chevy Pickup. Chunks of faded red paint was already flaking off the older tank onto the wood-planked truck bed. The still-bright paint of the other gas can sparkled in the July sun. Next came two wooden oars, a Danforth anchor, bailing bucket, life jackets, food for three days, camp gear, spare clothes, and Bilbo, our lead dog.

Bilbo found a place in the truck bed as far away from the gas cans as possible. As the husky twitched away mosquitoes with his ears, Susan climbed onto the passenger side of the truck's bench seat. I slid behind the wheel and peered through a filthy windshield for traffic coming down Sixth Avenue. It was five o'clock on a Friday night in Bethel and the way to Brown Slough looked clear.

The truck's straight-six-cylinder engine banged to life after I pressed the floor starter button with my rubber-soled boot. I was always a little surprised when it started. Keeping the truck alive required friends with knowledge of where the abandoned Chevy trucks were located in the Bethel seawall. When no longer wanted, Bethel cars or trucks were pushed over the riverbank to join the other wrecks slowing down river erosion. This seawall provided needed spare parts for still operating vehicles. My truck's original three-on-the tree column shifter had been replaced with a four-on-the floor transmission mined from the seawall. When the drive shaft wore out, a previous owner had substituted a slightly longer one

About to drive the '57 Chevy loaded with dogs
and sled to a dry tundra trail
Bethel, Alaska 1983

from another Chevy. It worked fine as long as you didn't drive more than twenty miles an hour. The differential would bang into the truck bed once your reached twenty-one.

The worm gear for the truck's steering was so loose that I had to start spinning the wheel at least fifty feet before each intersection to make a turn. I was already turning it to the left as I let out the clutch and eased into first gear. The truck shuddered and tried to dive off the road and onto the tundra. A spin of the steering wheel to the right kept us on the road. We turned onto Main and rattled our way to the Brown Slough Bridge.

The stern of our sixteen-foot aluminum skiff was floating on the waters of Brown Slough when we arrived. I bought it last summer to replace my leaky wooden river skiff named the "Just Barely." Last night, when the high tide had made the slough navigable, I had moved the skiff three winding miles from its usual tie up spot in Alligator Acres Subdivision to the bridge. Sunday afternoon, when we plan to return, water in the slough should be high enough for me to drive the skiff to its home anchorage.

As I loaded gas and gear into the skiff, Susan went to Dundu's place for a takeaway order of burgers and fries. Dundu's Korean wife was a great hand with the burgers. I pocketed the Chevy's ignition key but left the truck unlocked. Bethel had less than ten miles of roads and streets and few places to hide an ancient Chevy pickup truck with "Bethel Migrant Workers" painted on the driver's side door.

Bilbo refused to leave the truck's bed, even after Susan placed a bag of Dundu burgers in the boat. I had to carry him into the skiff. There he skulked over to a broad, wooden box with low sides where he would stay until we reached the berry picking grounds. I had to step over him to reach the back of the skiff. Susan pushed us out, climbed over the bow gunwale, and took a seat near the front of the skiff. It never occurred to either us that she should drive.

While we floated down the slough toward the Kuskokwim River, I stood, faced the skiff's 35-horse Evinrude kicker, and gripped the handle of its starting cord. After two pulls, it purred awake. Sitting down, I slipped ear protectors on and used the motor's throttle arm to steer us up river. With a Dundu burger in my right hand, I used my left to twist the throttle arm, giving the kicker enough gas to overcome the river's current. Forward momentum lifted the skiff until it skimmed over the river's surface.

Squinting against sun reflecting off the river, I steered around a sandbar and into Steamboat Slough. Cottonwood trees lining both banks blocked the wind so the slough waters were flat-ass calm. The skiff slalomed around the curves at top speed. Bilbo hunkered into his wooden box on each turn.

The sound of our kicker echoed off the banks and announced our exit from the slough to a flock of artic terns brooding their young on a nearby sandbar. I muttered an apology as the fierce little birds rose in a cloud above their nests.

Small river swells struck the boat after we passed the tern's sandbar. A mile upriver, I beached the boat at the base of a tundra-covered bluff. Bilbo leaped out of the boat. Susan pulled it onto the beach. I tied the Danforth anchor to the end of the bow line and kicked its flukes into the sand.

We carried camping gear and food up the thirty-foot-high bluff and on to a spot flat enough for our tent. We staked out the tent, taking care not to crush too many blueberries in the process. After we filled the tent with sleeping bags and self-inflating pads, I carried my meter-long Swedish bow saw to the beach to cut up a green birch tree that had washed up on the beach during the spring breakup flood. Its wood would perfume the house when it burned in our stove next winter.

Designed for efficiency, not safety, the naked teeth of a new Swede saw blade could rip through driftwood almost as fast as a chain saw. Dulled by previously cutting through silt-covered logs, my saw blade bounced off the birch's bark as I started my first cut. Mosquitoes bit the sensitive flesh along the edge of my baseball cap. Others tried to crawl into my eyes, ears and nostrils. Frustrated, skin burning with fresh bug bites, I drove the saw forward. It jumped off the birch log and cut deep into my left thumb knuckle.

I was too stunned to feel pain but shock didn't blind me to the blood. It formed a red lake in the deep gash then flowed over my thumb and onto the white birch bark. I crushed up a willow leaf and stuffed the cut with it and climbed up the bluff. At the top I fainted, toppling onto the tundra like a windfallen tree.

Accident prone, I always carried a trauma-ready first aid kit. After retrieving it from the tent, I tore the wrapper off several gauze squares with my teeth and pressed them on the wound with my right hand. They slowed the blood flow long enough for me to bite off a strip of adhesive tape and use it to press the gauze over the wound. By this time Susan had arrived with a concerned Bilbo. The husky lowered its ears to half-mast as he watched us pack up the tent and camp gear.

With my left hand raised skyward to keep the wound from reopening, I carried gear to the boat. It didn't take long for Susan and I to repack it. The adhesive tape securing my makeshift loosened. Blood started seeping from the wound. Worried about infection, and wondering whether we would make it to the Bethel Hospital before it closed for the night, I applied direct pressure on the cut to staunch the fresh bleeding.

The wound prevented me from using my left hand to steer the boat. I could have gripped the throttle with my right hand but I needed it to keep pressure on the still bleeding cut. Susan, who had never before driven the boat, had to get us to Bethel.

We knew many women on the river who could drive a skiff better than me. I had taught two of them what I knew about running their own skiffs. But it never occurred to Susan nor I that she should learn how to bring the Starcraft up on step or make it slice through boat wakes at a forty-five- degree angle. It wasn't that she couldn't do it. She just never wanted to learn. That night she had no choice.

Pulling up the hood of her old high school sweatshirt, Susan secured the noise-cancelling muffs over her ears and stood to face the outboard motor. Arms strong from hauling salmon and carrying cans of boat gas, she had no problems pull starting the kicker. Getting the hang of steering took her longer. But soon she was holding a straight course down river.

I was raised by a strong-minded woman who worked as a phlebotomist for the U.S. Public Health Service at a time when it was almost a boys-only club. Her wheat-ranching father died when she was eight. She watched her widowed mother hold on to the ranch in Montana through the Depression years and still manage to feed a chicken dinner every Sunday to her hard-scrabbled cousins. In Mom's house there were no boy chores or girl chores, just shared chores.

As dusk followed sunset that night on the Kuskokwim River, I was glad Mom wasn't in the skiff to question how Susan and I had settled into an old fashioned, if not sexist division of labor in our Bethel lives.

My left hand throbbed as we flew past the tern's sand bar and moved down river to Straight Slough. It provided the fastest route to Bethel. Susan had no problem piloting the skiff around a sand bar and into the slough. Not having to search ahead for snags, I watched a woman cutting fish in front of her family's fish camp tent. The drawstring of her cotton kuspuk hood was pulled tight to keep out swarming mosquitoes. She would be joining me tonight in the hospital emergency room if while distracted by mosquitoes, she cut herself with the wickedly-sharp uluk she used to slice silver salmon sides away from the fish's backbone.

After swerving around the sand bar that partially blocked the lower end of Straight Slough, we sped past the shacks of Louse Town. At the mouth of Brown Slough, Susan eased down the throttle and slid onto the beach in front of the '57 Chevy truck.

We transferred gear and the dog from skiff to truck and secured the boat anchor. Even though she had just done a good job piloting the skiff, she refused to drive the truck because of its dicey steering. After wrapping my wound with more adhesive tape, I started the truck and switched on its weak headlights. We crawled the miles to our house and returned Bilbo to his dog house. He disappeared into it before Susan and I had climbed back into the truck cab.

I muscled the old truck onto Main Street and turned right onto Eddie Hoffman Highway. Named after the town's traditional chief, it was the only paved road in town. Keeping our speed to under twenty miles-per-hour, I coaxed the Chevy up the highway and into an empty hospital parking lot. The front door of the hospital was locked so we went to the ambulance entrance and looked for the on-call physician's assistant. Roger, the resident bone setting expert led us to his work station. He showed excitement, rather than sympathy while he removed my makeshift bandaging and injected my thumb with a local anesthetic.

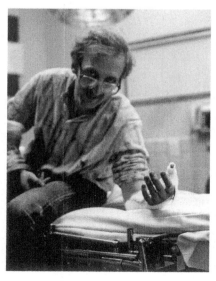

I could see a flash of white bone after he flushed dried blood and chunks of crushed willow leaf from my wound. After that I looked away. Roger used an oversized syringe to wash down the cut with Betadine. While chatting away like a man with too few friends, he stitched a repair of my thumb ligament, sutured up the ragged cut, and used a steel splint and an elastic

Getting stiches in the Bethel hospital

bandage to immobilize my thumb. Handing me a small bottle of aspirin, Roger warned me that I might lose some function in the thumb.

My immobilized thumb didn't prevent me from sawing, splitting and stacking firewood that summer. I could still use our 50-fathom drift net to catch enough silver salmon for the winter. I could even drive the '57 Chevy truck. But I couldn't hold on to the dog sled when exercising our team. They needed to train. The following winter we would be running in a 300-hundred-mile dog race. Each day that summer, Susan hitched four dogs at a time to a cobbled-together wooden cart and let them pull her up and down the silt streets of Bethel. By September, my hand had healed enough for me to take over the training.

After work each day, I loaded eight dogs and a sled into the Chevy's bed and drove through Housing, past the laundromat and the high school to the dump. From there the dogs pulled me and the sled up the Akiachak Bluffs Trail. Years of snow machine and dog team traffic had compressed the tundra under the trail and broken down the little grass islands called tussocks that would have made it impossible to run dogs on the trail without snow cover. The trail provided a challenging but usable path until it ended at the edge of a flooded ravine.

A snow machine or wheeled all-terrain vehicle would have bogged down on the fragile trail. The dogs did not. As they toned their winter muscles trotting on the spongy ground, I helped the sled along by jamming a foot onto the trail, pushing it backwards, and swinging it forward for another push.

As the dogs and I fell into rhythm, I'd swat mosquitoes and try to remember how the trail looked in winter after all the greens had faded to brown, blueberry plants were reduced to leafless sticks, and nothing flew in the sky but airplanes and ravens.

Early the previous winter, before the first snowfall and after an arctic cold snap brought sub-zero temperatures over night, I hitched up a small team of dogs and let them pull me down this trail and then up a newly frozen creek. We traveled over ice so clear that we could see muskrats swimming beneath the sled runners. Only a dog team could travel over such bare ice. Few mushers were willing to risk a slip-and-fall injury to a dog so they waited for snow to cover the trail. But they were training to build up speed for the winter races. Last year, I just wanted to see what was around the next bend and know that it was not going to be another dog team or snow machine.

We never saw another dog team or hunters that summer on the Akiachak Bluffs Trail. But long-tailed jaegers glided over the green tundra, which sometimes moved with mice. Cessna prop planes hauled people, mail, and freight over our heads. Years after I left the Kuskokwim, moose started moving down river to browse on willows along the trail. But the summer I used the trail to train up the dogs, sandhill cranes were the largest animals we saw.

One September afternoon a small "V" of sandhill cranes flew toward us. I heard their rusty-hinge calls before spotting the long-necked birds. Rather than climb out of gun range, as they usually do when flying over men, the cranes eased toward us. They flew in a tight circle low over the team. After three or four loops, they climbed high enough to pass over Bethel without drawing a shot. I told Bilbo to turn around by shouting, "gee haw."

I felt like God had just granted the prayer I had made each time cranes flew thousands of feet above my head—let them come close enough for me to see if they really have blue eyes like the Yup'ik story tellers claimed. One of my favorite Yup'ik stories was "How the Crane Got its Blue Eyes." But the eye color of the cranes that circled my dog team that day didn't matter. I didn't even think to check. The magic was in the closeness, that the cranes chose to close the distance.

It was wilderness magic, usually only present where the animals are ignorant of man's violence—remote waters where seals hitch rides on the back deck of kayaks or old growth forests where hummingbirds land on your shoulder and deer cross rivers to investigate a backpacker's camp.

After I watched the cranes fly over town and then down river, we headed back to the '57 Chevy. Without having mastered the steering of that old truck, I could never have driven the dog team under cranes that mistook them for something of their tundra world rather than of man's.

Pounding out the miles

Elegy

— After "Elegy" by Wendell Berry

1

Elias taught me how to set a net for kings,
the richest, tastiest salmon.

He stood in the bow of his plank-bottom skiff,
lead line in one hand, float line in the other,
rhythmically tossing both up and out over
the river. The lead line hit the surface
like a series of fist blows and sank five fathoms.
The other line, with its string of white floats
formed a 300 foot long smile across
the current. When enough kings ensnared
themselves in the web wall, Elias pulled
the net, coiling the webbing carefully
into a galvanized washtub, used
the net's tension to ease salmon
from the web.

2

Miles and years away from the river, salmon and the silent ghosts
of fisherman swim through my nightmares. Some ghosts float
out of bodies that had tumbled from skiffs into the Kuskokwim,
the smell of whiskey still stinking up their boats. Others emerge
from holes in weak river ice or from bodies frozen on the tundra.
Elias dies in his sleep.

3

In my dream, Elias' plank bottom skiff slaps through chop.
His spirit throttles back until the boat drifts and the engine murmurs.
He's not the fit fisherman of memory; He's an 80-year-old widower
with hands softer than his voice.

"You should drive," he says, "you can throw the net."

4

So they will let me sleep,
Elias, the veteran eulogizer celebrates my ghosts:
Nicolai once dropped a swan with an impossible shot
to break the spring famine of his family,

Junior always made us laugh by mimicking ptarmigan
during Eskimo dances at the National Guard Armory,

Bummy fed his mother all winter with snared rabbits,
dried salmon and his fall moose,

Tuntu hauled drinking water ice for his mom, chopped
firewood for his Uppa between stints in jail.

All the river's ghosts lived and loved
and were loved even by those they hurt,

Any of them could have been your friend,
uncovered tiny tundra beauties.

Every one of them could have taught you
the trick of mourning by remembrance.

Dust

We packed the skiff with everything needed for a blueberry-picking trip. Susan and our lead dog, Bilbo sat in the bow. As it did on every entry, the skiff jerked when nosed into the Kuskokwim River from Brown Slough. Sitting at the stern with my right hand on the motor's tiller, I turned upriver from Bethel and headed toward the Straight Slough shortcut. There was little wind, just enough to raise clouds of fine dust from Louse Town's riverside streets.

We skimmed over opaque waters brown with glacier silt, an avenue for homebound salmon and other unseen objects. We might be passing over the body of the upriver guy who had drowned two months earlier. Returning to his home village from Bethel after a trip to the bootlegger, he fell from his high-sided wooden skiff somewhere along the route we were about to take. A man from his village spotted the empty skiff circling, a spilled bottle of bootlegged booze on the floorboards. Such a simple thing would have saved the man's life—not opening the bottle until he got home. He must have tossed away the bottle cap before taking his first drink.

Flowing alcohol kept my law practice humming. With a few exceptions, all my criminal clients were drunk when they committed their crimes. None of the parents I represented in child protection cases would have lost their kids if they could have stayed sober. Frustrated by alcohol's destructive powers and emotionally strained by working as a defense attorney on a recent series of child sexual abuse cases, I needed healing time on the tundra.

We moved with speed upriver before passing the summer fish camps along Straight Slough. Some had big wall tents while others provided unpainted plywood cabins for shelter. On this Saturday in July, smoke rose from most of the dwellings, even those owned by folks with jobs in Bethel. Every fish camp had a smoke house fashioned out of weathered plywood, each filled with drying king salmon strips and dog salmon filets. In front of one, a woman with the hood of her cotton kuspuk pulled tight around her face against mosquitoes was cutting fish. One half-naked child chased another one past her. After making a sweeping turn around the sandbar that guarded the top end of Straight Slough, I returned to the river and steered between the western shore and a large sandbar. A thin cloud of sharp-tailed terns rose from the bar when we passed.

Minutes later I spotted our goal---a "C" shaped bluff cut by the river from a low silt hill. I pointed it out to Susan, who had her back turned away from the wind that blew over the boat's bow. We always camped there, often during berry picking season, even after the incident where I nearly cut my thumb off there with a Swede saw.

Pleased that no net reached into the eddy swirling at the bluff's upriver edge, I steered for a place just downriver of it. Bilbo jumped onto the beach before we came to a stop. Susan followed, taking the bowline with her. As she kicked the anchor flukes into the sand, I unloaded the boat. She climbed up a rough trail in the bluff, berry bucket in hand, dog at her heels, as I secured one end of the net to a clump of beachside alder. While Susan picked berries, I set the net to catch some early run silver salmon.

Before joining Susan on top of the bluff, I scanned the Kuskokwim, its surface now empty of moving things. No village skiffs headed home with drums of boat gas and bags of groceries bought at too high a price from a Bethel store. Only the willows colonizing a mid-channel sandbar moved, leaves flashing from dark to light green and back in a light breeze. Above, the sky was empty of noisy prop planes. The stress built up during the previous week's jury trial started to dissipate in the welcomed quiet.

Taking the path Susan used, I scrambled up to where a fringe of tundra hung like poorly trimmed bangs over the bluff top. Living plant roots fastened onto a mat of the dead pioneers that had sent their roots into a dune of drying river silt. Above grew a miniature forest of dwarf birch, Labrador tea, wildflowers, and berries. It smelled like acrid river silt mixed with compost and the scent of wild rose blossoms. I searched for Susan and Bilbo but saw only a rolling plain broken here and there by scrub willows. Figuring that Susan had found good picking in a hidden patch, I stopped looking and dropped onto tundra heavy with dark blue fruit where nothing provided mosquitoes shelter from the wind.

When picking became automatic, my mind washed the week's laundry. It sorted through the emotions and memories from the trial in which I'd defended a man charged with sexual abuse of his 5-year-old niece. The jury had strained to hear the child quietly say that her uncle had climbed into her bed and touched her private parts with his. It was easier to hear the doctor describe the slight reddening of her perineum. My client didn't take the stand. The jury took half an hour to convict.

An afternoon of berry picking or even a long sled dog ride at 40 below usually tamped down memories of what I did and failed to do for clients. I'd forget the tearful or angry victim interview, awful wounds camouflaged by dry medical report jargon, forensic photographs of a child's physical damage, the greater injury revealed in the victim's eyes. On this day, I could not bury my memories of the damaged child.

I moved from the rich berry patch to another trying to escape the memories of that trial. This time, the berry patch magic did not work.

I breathed deeply of clean, silt-free air. Urging my mind to change the subject, I thought about Bethel before dust, before oil flowed from the Arctic Slope to Valdez. The new oil brought the state money to fund fancy buildings in Anchorage and pay for Bethel's growing miles of raised silt roads. The older, thin roads never quite dried out, making driving an adventure, but they produced little dust. In those days, few people had cars so we waved at the cars we knew, even when distance or a dirty windshield obscured our view of the driver.

The new, drier roads encouraged more car ownership. Infused with oil money, government agencies and non-profit corporations added new jobs. Bethel's population swelled as did the need for new housing. The city had to build silt roads to connect new house subdivisions where houses were elevated above the tundra by a pad of river silt. Soon, every breeze carried airborne silt that settled in your eyes, lungs, and on your clothes.

Unlike the mosquitoes and gnats, the dust continued to plague us after the fall's killing frosts.

I thought about a recent client interview of the parents of neglected children. The state had taken the kids away because they spent their food and clothing money on bingo and booze. The lawyer's ethics code guaranteed them my loyalty without judgment. I had to work hard for the return of their kids, as I did the first time the social workers took them away.

When I started to wonder whether my work mattered, I walked away from another promising berry patch to look for Susan. Maybe her presence would help. A fast picker, she had her bucket three-quarters full by the time I found her. I imagined the pie and jam it would make and wondered if the store still had any of that high butterfat vanilla ice cream.

My efforts in the new patch harvested berries but not peace, so I stretched out on the tundra. The spongy ground was wet but my rain gear kept me dry. I sank in until eye level with a dwarf birch forest. Normally the tundra's energy healed like warm rays of spring sunlight.

Bilbo stretched and wandered over to drop onto a nearby patch of tundra. We had long been close, just as a farmer and plough horse are close. The old lead dog had once led the team and me through a whiteout storm when flying snow masked all reference points. Unlike his master, Bilbo never suffered long from stress in his life. A few caresses of the soft fur near his ears would clear away his clouds. As he slept, I tried not to think of his death or wonder who would lead me through whiteouts when he was gone.

The wind dropped, allowing a plague of mosquitoes to settle over us. It was time to go. After loading the boat, I pulled the net. One male silver, chrome sides still ocean bright, struggled in the web. With dinner in the boat, I returned to shore to pick up Susan and Bilbo. She hopped in and called for the dog to join us. He backed up slowly until firm against the bluff face. His eyes flared wide in fear then narrowed as he slinked down the beach. When I climbed over the boat gunwale toward him, he darted away, his long lush tail wrapped protectively under his privates. He had earned more of my patience than I could offer him that day. Standing in a cloud of biting bugs, I urged him to "come." He moved farther down the beach. I turned my back, then quickly reversed and lunged but he was too nimble. We danced up and down the beach to the tune of my curses until I hopped back into the boat, made one last plea, and then pushed back from the beach.

When I started the motor, Bilbo barked, then ran to the crease made in the beach sand by our boat's keel. He even took a few tentative steps into the river. Encouraged, I motored back and asked him to join us. Bilbo ran down the beach. After pushing off and returning a few times to the sand, I swung the motor tiller until the boat pointed toward Bethel and opened the throttle. Bilbo loped down the beach on a parallel course until running out of sand. He leaped into the water and swam toward town. We motored over and plucked his streaming body from the river.

Had Bilbo tried to keep me on the berry patch until healed or did he just want to distance himself from my frustration? It was probably the latter. His sled dog performance rose and fell with my mood.

After the brief calm that encouraged our departure from the bluff, the wind rose again, blowing upriver against the outgoing tide. We bounced into every resulting wave. Looking for calmer water, I dropped into Steamboat Slough, a winding route named for two paddle wheel boats that had been rotting for years on the banks. The skiff tilted into each turn, some coming in quick succession. Susan and I leaned into them like riders on a rollercoaster while Bilbo lowered his center of gravity on the bottom of the boat.

Returning to the main river, I throttled back so we could enjoy the evening sun reflecting off the red metal sides of the Louse Town cold storage and raising a glare on the windows of unpainted riverside cabins. Most people would consider Bethel and the cold storage plain or even ugly but the scene usually made me smile. I loved the sheet metal and plywood Bethel, not for its buildings but for the people who lived in them and had made us feel welcome.

Yup'ik cultural rules mandated consideration of others. Prey animals watched how you treated people in need and whether you shoveled a path through snow for your elders. Let the snow pile up and the animals gave themselves to one better behaved. The rules required patience. After entering a Yup'ik home, even when invited in to provide legal help, I was expected to drink tea quietly until my host was ready to ask her question.

The rules demanded care of helpless strangers like me. When I had a cold while visiting a Yup'ik village, an older widow cared for me. She made sure that children weren't exposed to my germs while she fed me seal soup rich with vitamin C. Watching the sunshine on Louse Town at the end of the berry-picking trip, I wondered if even people so rich in kindness could keep me on the river.

Above Bethel, a rolling brown cloud of river silt crawled along as if auditioning for an Oklahoma dust bowl movie. It had already enveloped the airport and housing areas between those areas and town. Soon it would make it even harder for people who couldn't escape their stress.

The next week I would walk through dust to advocate at child protection hearings; defend teenagers charged with rape or arson; interview yet another man in jail, nice and polite now that he was sober, about his child sexual abuse charge. During that visit, there would be quiet while he read, without obvious reaction, the criminal complaint. I would try not to see him as a monster but as a man who shared his first seal in the way required by tradition, hauled water for his elders, prayed hard in church; a man who tossed away the cap of his bootlegged whiskey bottle, drank it dry with other nice men and women who also believed that this time the monsters had all escaped from the booze before their first sip. Then he'd put the charging document on the table and slide it to me, maybe nod his head or whisper, "I don't remember." He'd ask if he could go home because his family needed fish, a moose, or winter firewood. I'd tell him there was a chance if he promised not to drink until the trial. He would promise that to me and then to the judge. If he kept his promise, I might secure him a shorter sentence but he would go to jail after a trial that he would lose after the jury heard his confession. He, like most others charged with crimes in Bethel, confessed.

Was I about to lose the ability to treat criminal defendants as the nice people they were, who did terrible things while drunk? Was I forgetting that my child abuse files did not describe days in the life of typical Yup'ik families? I feared the sleepless nights sure to come when dog sledding, fishing, and berry picking no longer worked. I needed to leave before losing myself in the dust.

F-----g Gussuck

Ambulance crews sometimes must see people at their worst. But just as stories told by paramedics in Los Angeles or New York cannot be used to define those communities, the brief ones told in this essay should not be used to draw a negative picture of the kind and generous Yup'ik people of Western Alaska.

During my tenth year in the Alaska bush town of Bethel, I worked the Fourth of July graveyard shift as a volunteer EMT on the fire department's ambulance. For most of the night, sunlight bounced off the walls of the firehouse bunkroom. I fell asleep at the start of the brief dusk period that passes for night during that sun rich time of the northern year. The disembodied voice of the dispatcher woke me with our first call to service—"Ambulance crew, respond to the small boat harbor. See the man injured in a three-wheeler accident." Immediately awake, I followed the professional paramedic into an ambulance. He drove to where a balloon-tired Honda all-terrain vehicle pinned a man to the silty road.

A middle aged Yup'ik woman, hair wild, hands covered with blood thickened by road silt, screamed over the man. After making sure she was uninjured, the paramedic checked the man, also Yup'ik, for vital signs. He told me to shine a light on the accident victim. A mask of blood covered his face. After I gasped, the paramedic said, "Cut on the scalp, right there at the hairline, always big bleeders." The man reported no distress except from the face wound, so we righted the three-wheeler, helped him sit up, and used sterile saline to clean his face. With direct pressure, the paramedic stopped the bleeding and applied a dressing. We helped the man into the ambulance. His companion, who never stopped screaming, "*Eee Li*," slapped the rear ambulance doors with her palms, leaving bloody handprints on the windows. She ran after the ambulance for a block, before doubling over, palms on knees. The metallic smell of fresh blood, whiskey and day old drinker's sweat filled the ambulance. After double clicking the radio microphone, the paramedic told a standby nurse at the hospital, "In bound with one patient, male, mid-forties, stable vitals, etoh [ethyl alcohol] involved. Estimated arrival ten minutes. Over."

Alcohol was involved in so much of my life on the Kuskokwim. The police reports for most of the clients of my law office stated that alcohol was involved in the underlying crime. People I knew and liked when sober were arrested or had their kids taken away for something they did during an alcoholic blackout. Some drowned or froze to death while drunk. The town was dry but many Bethelites had beer and booze shipped in on flights from Anchorage. You didn't have to be Yup'ik to develop a drinking problem. Plenty of gussucks, as many of the white folk on the river like me were called, drank to destruction.

I would have gone home after we dropped the head wound off at the hospital, but I needed volunteer hours to keep up my EMT certification. In a month, Susan and I would move 130 miles up the Kuskokwim River to Aniak and 130 miles away from the nearest paramedic. The village had a health aide and we would be living across a slough from the health aide's office. Current life-saving knowledge turned out to be needed by the community. One spring, when broken ice damned the river and cut off our neighborhood from the rest of Aniak, I was asked to serve as acting health aide. The next day, I had to walk through the flooded community to check on a small, injured child.

We went out on six runs that night, but I remember nothing about the second, third, fourth or fifth ones. The sixth ambulance summons came at seven in the morning. "Possible suicide attempt, woman, age 25, self-reported taking entire bottle of Tylenol." In bright sunlight we drove to a recently painted ranch style house in a well-kept subdivision. The paramedic knocked on the door.

"Go away you f-----g gussucks."

Carrying a quart of saline and a stainless steel bowl manufactured for mixing bread dough, I followed the paramedic into the house. He did all the talking. A woman, trim in Land's End knit top and fitted pants, thick black hair recently trimmed into a Dorothy Hamill bowl cut, tottered from the door and said, "Let me die you f-----g gussucks."

This squelched any desire I had to speak but not the experienced paramedic who responded, "Yes mam. Did you take a quantity of Tylenol?"

"Yes."

"How many mam?"

"The whole bottle."

"When was this mam?"

"Just let me die."

"When did you take the medication mam?"

"I don't remember you f-----g gussuck."

"Mam, please drink this. It's just salt water."

Taking the bottle, she said, "f-----g gussuck."

Between breaks, which she filled with "let me die f-----g gussuck," she downed the entire quart of saline.

"Mam that is going to make you empty your stomach. Please catch the contents in this bowl. It is important."

"F-----g gussuck," she mumbled, then did as he asked.

The patient and I rode to the hospital in the back of the ambulance. It bumped along a gravel road past a patch of tundra crisscrossed by boardwalks called Pinky's Park. Through the dried blood handprints on the rear window, I could see volunteers stock a face painting booth and some food stands. The former contents of the patient's stomach swirled in the mixing bowl that I cradled in my lap. When we stopped at an intersection, I counted 30 intact white tablets in the consommé of saline and stomach acid. The patient muttered, "I just wanted to die, f-----g gussucks." The paramedic reported on the radio, "In bound with 25-year-old female, vitals stable, recently consumed bottle of Tylenol, suicide ideation, etoh involved. Over."

Angry and tired, I could never have acted with the calm efficiency shown by the paramedic. *How many times does someone have to call you a f-----g gussuck before it stops bothering you?* I wondered as we pulled up to the hospital.

I know the bloody handprints on the ambulance helped me remember details of the three-wheeler accident. Was it the strength of my emotional reaction or the suicide's beauty that allowed me to recall the way her thick hair bounced against the smooth skin of her cheeks when she yelled, "f-----g gussuck"?

PART TWO

Aniak

Dictator

Since it was weighed down by my partner Susan, 20 gallons of boat gas, suitcases, camp gear, a dog sled, wheel barrow, and a three-speed J.C. Penny bicycle, I couldn't push my skiff off Bethel's new boat ramp. Normally, we would have loaded the boat at Brown Slough's tiny beach near our house rather than haul everything down to Bethel's new boat harbor ramp. But almost overloaded with gear, the boat wouldn't have made the three mile cruise to the river without getting repeatedly hung up in creek side brush. After Susan climbed over the gear to stand near the outboard motor, the bow lifted enough for me to finally push the boat into the harbor waters.

Before it could crash into another boat, I scrambled to the back of the skiff as Susan moved forward to take a seat on the middle thwart. I waved goodbye to the friends who had helped us load up the skiff and steered toward the Kuskokwim River. One of them, a fan of Woodie Guthrie and John Steinbeck, shouted, "If you had Granny and a rocking chair you might be the Joads."

The next night, if we didn't run out of gas or luck, we would beach the skiff in front of our new home in Aniak, 130 miles upriver from Bethel. Two days after that, on July 1, 1986, I'd start work as the Aniak magistrate. Susan and I had met almost 10 years before in Bethel. That's eight years longer than most non-Yup'ik people live there. We still loved the kindness and teasing of the Native people. But dust storms and my stressful legal caseload were driving us out of town. Susan and I decided

Dan's cabin across the slough from Aniak

to live for two years in Aniak, a small, upriver village before moving to Anchorage or another Alaskan city.

My new magistrate job would only take four hours a day, from 10 A.M. to 2 P.M. I expected to sleep in every morning and spend the afternoons dog mushing in winter and fishing or gardening in summer. For centuries, the bodies of hundreds of thousands of spawned out salmon had rotted in the waters surrounding Aniak. During the breakup flood each summer, water filled with the proteins and chemicals released by the dead fish soaked into village ground. It was a great place for vegetable farming.

We had started moving bits and pieces of our life to the village of 300 people the prior winter. A friend who worked as a water truck delivery driver used his four-wheel-drive Dodge to haul my 440 Kawasaki snow machine and sleds up an informal road on the frozen Kuskokwim River to Aniak. The road meandered from bank to bank around sections of open water and jumbles of ice slabs. Ninety miles upriver forests of white spruce and birch replaced the cottonwoods and willows that lined the river for the first part of the trip. A few miles further we got our first glimpse of the Russian Mountains. That night my friend and I stayed in the Aniak Lodge's one good room—the one with two beds, carpeting and a door that opened on a bathroom with running water.

In early summer Susan and I mailed our winter clothes, sled dog harnesses, and 50-pound bags of dogfood general delivery to the Aniak post office.

Before winding down my law practice, I had helped a family obtain an adoption decree in exchange for a Yamaha three-wheeler and a Grumman freight canoe. A barge pushed upriver by a river boat delivered both to Aniak.

Another client paid off his legal bill by flying our eight sled dogs to Aniak. After the pilot removed all but the front two seats in the plane, I installed the tie-out cable I usually used for securing the dogs when camping. Each dog spent the flight clipped to the cable, which kept them out of trouble but didn't prevent them from looking out one of the plane's windows. I was worried about how they would handle the flight. But they were all calm when we landed in Aniak. After leaving the dogs in the care of friend, I flew back to Bethel in the empty plane. The next day Susan and I started upriver in the boat.

We had spent a lot of time on the lower river to driftnet for salmon, pick berries, fish for pike, or just to decompress on the tundra. We'd sped past Akiachak and beached the boat in front of Kwethluk and Akiak. We knew that part of the river. But once we passed Akiak, we would have to rely on knowledge from stories told by friends from upriver villages and forty-year-old government maps.

After draining the first six-gallon tank of gas, we camped for the night on a silt island in the Tuluksak Flats, just past Akiak Village. Our boots sunk to mid-calve in the mud when we hopped off the skiff, but there was enough firm ground above the beach for tenting. Mosquitoes drove us into the tent after we finished a meal of roasted kielbasa sausage and green apples. We slept well even though it never got dark.

After the sun dried out the nylon sides of out tent the next morning, we broke camp and worked our way through the flats—a slow-water section of the river full of sand bars and false channels. Once, a big flat-bottom river skiff passed us, loaded down with kids, drums of gas and boxes of groceries. After that we had the water to ourselves as we slipped past the mouth of the Tuluksak River

Sunset on the Aniak River beach

and on toward Lower Kalskag. Seeing the beach on the western bank of the Tuluksak River reminded me of the four hours that I had rested Bilbo and my other sled dogs there the first night of the Kusko 300 race. I had to break up a nasty fight that eventually knocked three of my dogs out of the race.

Twenty miles downriver from Lower Kalskag, the speed of the river current climbed, slowing our progress. If it had slipped into neutral, we would drift back down river. The bars and river bottom here were covered with gravel rather than the glacial silt of the Tuluksak Flats. I couldn't relax even though it was easier to find the right channels. One run-in with a gravel bar would destroy the outboard prop. I only had one spare.

Sometimes the channel undercut steep-sided silt banks topped with 50-foot-high white spruce trees or took us past semicircle meadows partially ringed with paper birch trees. River erosion had carried away the birch that once has blocked the meadows from river view.

Ninety miles into the trip we reached the Yup'ik village of Lower Kalskag—a collection of log houses gathered around a traditional Russian Orthodox Church. The church's three blue-domes sparkled in the summer air. Our last can of gas was almost empty. I worried that we wouldn't have enough to make it the three miles to a Moravian missionary trading post that sold boat gas.

When a fast moving-skiff approached from downriver, I flagged it down. It was driven by a Yup'ik friend on his way to a village upriver from Aniak to spend the Fourth of July with his family. After teasing us for looking like Okies, he handed over a three-gallon jug of boat gas.

Last winter, when he learned that I was taking the Aniak magistrate job, he warned me not to be a potato with a penis on it. "I mean don't be a dictator," he said after reading the puzzled expression on my face. "You are going to have a lot of power in that job, don't abuse it." Later, the Bethel Superior Court judge told me to enjoy the job because in the village I would be "The law west of the Pecos."

My friend and the judge were both right. With the exception of the Alaska State Troopers stationed there, I would be the sole representative of state government in Aniak. I would be able to hold trials, impose jails sentences, order spouses to stay away from their families, and declare deaths to be homicides, which could lead to murder charges. I would perform marriages and sign marriage dissolution decrees. The nearest place for my customers to obtain legal advice would always be 130 river miles away. If I wasn't careful, I could become a dictator.

By the time we met on the river near Lower Kalskag, my friend must have decided that I would not abuse my authority. Otherwise, he wouldn't have given me the boat gas. After pouring his gift into my almost empty gas can, we motored on and beached the skiff near the Ausdahl missionary small grocery store. Mrs. Ausdahl had just made several gallons of high bush cranberry jelly, which was setting up in pint jars. She stacked the jars on a window sill until the only light reaching the store had to travel through rose-colored jelly.

I wanted to stay in the store, which smelled of sugar and berry juice, but we still had thirty miles of river to climb before reaching Aniak. I followed the missionary to his gas pump on the river and filled up two six-gallon tanks.

A line of low mountains lined the west side of the river above Lower Kalskag. Wind cutting through gaps in the hills raised bad chop on the water. We powered through the waves, passing homesteads and fish camps. At ten in the evening, we pulled even with Aniak. A high earthen dike blocked most of the village from our view. Beached boats and floating rafts with fish cutting tables lined the river bank. Children with spinning rods fished for the trout attracted to the fish cutting rafts by salmon guts.

Aniak village sat on an island bordered by the Kuskokwim River and Aniak slough. The "A" frame cabin that we would rent was on the other side of a small stream from the village. In low water years our neighbors could walk across the slough to the village. The summer we moved to Aniak, we needed a boat to cross it.

Two mud bars guarded the entrance to Aniak Slough. I managed to run aground on both of them. Since it was warm and sunny, most of the village were doing something on the beach when we arrived. They all stopped to watch their new magistrate pole his overloaded skiff off each mud bar.

After unloading the skiff and checking on the dogs, Susan and I rolled out our sleeping bags on the "A" frame's bed platform. The cabin had no toilet, shower, or even a water tap. It did have a giant Riteway wood stove that could burn four-foot lengths of spruce. I would have to cut five cords of wood each winter to feed the beast. I'd have to haul drinking water into the cabin and our human waste out of it. We'd cook our meals on a tiny propane stove and store the left overs in a college-dorm sized refrigerator. It was a make-do place, and you couldn't drive a car to it.

Before turning in, Susan and I walked out to the slough bluff for another look at the village. From there we could see over the top of the dike to the Lodge, Post Office, and Auntie Mary Nicolai School. We could also see the Anchorage bound 737 jet taxing down the village's mile long runway. After reaching the end of the runway, the pilot did a "U" turn, cranked down the flaps and hit the throttle. A huge dust cloud trailed the plane down the runway. The wind lifted the cloud into the air and pushed it across the slough. Fine silt drifted from the cloud into our hair and onto our clothes. We knew then that as long as we lived on the river, there would always be dust.

A Little Traction

A tired looking Cessna 185 prop plane rattled to a stop next to a Bethel air charter service shack. The shack smelled of gasoline, burned coffee and cigarette smoke. Before the plane arrived, a thirty-six-year-old version of myself had been thumbing through a year-old copy of *Reader's Digest*. Carol, an in-court clerk sat a few feet away on a creaky office chair. Tucked between us on the concrete floor was a court system sample case containing Carol's portable cassette recorder, log sheets, pens, and my black judge robe. We didn't need to pack food because someone in the village we were flying to had promised to give us dried salmon, pilot biscuits, and tea.

The pilot opened the office door and without entering shouted, "You folks ready for your charter to Tuluksak?" I could barely hear him over the sound of a landing aircraft. We stood without answering and followed the pilot to his plane. Carol took a seat behind him, letting me have the co-pilot's seat.

I don't remember what the pilot looked like but he was probably young and White. This was 1987. Then, almost all bush pilots were. After making sure that we had fastened our seatbelts, the pilot pointed to the back of the plane and said, "Emergency gear and beacon in the tail, any questions?" He throttled the engine to life before we could answer. I wished, as I always did at this point of in a bush flight, that I had brought ear plugs.

We taxied down the runway as the pilot radioed the Bethel Tower that he was about to fly to the Kuskokwim River village of Tuluksak with three souls on board. I jammed my fingers into my ears when the pilot snapped the plane onto the runway and pushed in the throttle. The plane rolled like a car down the tarmac, bounced into the air, back onto the runway and finally into the air.

A thousand feet up, the pilot throttled back and eased back in his seat. I looked down at the fish camps just upriver from Bethel. It was summer so drying salmon, dark red in color, weighed down driftwood racks in front of the camp cabins. For the twelve and half years that I lived on the river, I never had my own fish camp. Outsiders didn't keep one.

When I took the Aniak magistrate job, I hadn't expected to spend much time in Bethel or in the Aniak Court. They had a magistrate in Bethel to cover their misdemeanor cases. But as soon after I moved upriver, the district attorney started bumping the Bethel magistrate from all criminal cases, so I had to fly down to Bethel every month to preside for several days over all the misdemeanor trials and sentencings.

The Kuskokwim River snaked through the tundra below us. I relaxed for the first time that day. I had spent most of it in court taking changes of plea and sentencing people who had beat up someone or committed some other misdemeanor while drunk. Many were repeat customers.

During afternoon arraignments, the district attorney and the public defender representing a Tuluksak man approached the bench. They asked that we all fly to his home village to conduct a preliminary hearing in the case. At the hearing the D.A. would have to prove that the state had enough evidence to establish that the defendant burned down a half-constructed community hall. If they couldn't convince me they had the evidence, I'd dismiss the case. We agreed to meet at the village bingo hall in the late afternoon to hold the hearing.

After flying over the villages of Akiachak, Kwethluk, and Akiak, the plane approached the Tuluksak airstrip. From inside the plane, the

Dan about to start one of many criminal hearings in the Bethel Superior Court Building

village runway seemed too small for landing. It looked like a tiny, dust generating rectangle floating on a sea of yellow-green tundra. The pilot looked bored as he adjusted the throttle and flaps and guided the plane toward the tiny airstrip. We bounced twice before stabilizing on the gravel runway and rolling to a stop. There were no buildings to see, just a muddy road leading into the village. The pilot pulled out a paperback novel and said he'd wait for our return.

When I flew into a village that had a resident policeman, he would give me a ride to the city council building or community hall for the hearing. But no police officer lived in Tuluksak, so there was no one at the airstrip to give Carol or me a ride to town. Villagers probably knew why I was in town but no one tried to meet us at the plane after it landed. This was fine with me. I needed some quiet time to think about the case since I had spent the whole day sending people in Bethel to jail. I didn't mind when Carol left me after a few minutes to spend time at a friend's house before the hearing. Soon, the black court robe that I carried in my little day pack would turn me from a Kuskokwim guy into a serious judge when I put it on.

People in the village were always busy when the salmon were running. I walked along a muddy village road that cut across tundra crowded with moss, tiny blueberry bushes, and six-inch-tall birch trees. While walking, I rubbed on mosquito repellant and thought about the arson case.

According to the paperwork filed by the D.A., the defendant, Alexie Nicolai downed a bottle of bootlegged whiskey, splashed gasoline on a partially constructed community hall, and lit it on fire. Awakened by the smell of burning wood, villagers tried to save the building. None were trained fire fighters. They did their best with what was available—five-gallon buckets and fire extinguishers—but they lost the community hall.

Mr. Nicolai admitted to an Alaska State Trooper that he had set the fire to keep the village kids from using the half-built building as a private place to huff gasoline. He had seen some grade school kids drag a six-gallon can of boat gas into the building, open the cap, and breathe in the fumes. He knew that huffing gave the kids an escape from their problems at home. It also caused irreversible brain damage. I knew that if the case went to trial, Mr. Nicolai's confession should be enough for the jury to convict him of Arson in the Second Degree, which was a class B Felony.

A superior court judge could then order him to spend up to ten years in jail. I was thankful that as a magistrate I wouldn't be asked to sentence Mr. Nicolai for the arson.

It was common during those years for a brace of Alaska State Troopers to fly from their headquarters in Bethel to a Yup'ik village like Tuluksak and arrest someone accused of assault during an alcohol blackout. They easily located the suspect asleep in his family's government-built house or drinking morning coffee at his Auntie's. Now sober, the suspect normally told the troopers that he couldn't remember what had happened the night before. He'd admit that his cousin, who reported the crime to the troopers, always told the truth. If the cousin said that he saw him shoot a neighbor at the prior night's home brew party, he must have done it.

If the troopers brought a large enough plane, the victim, the bullet hole in his arm cleaned and bandaged by the village health aide, might fly back to Bethel with the suspect. The gunshot victim would return home in a few days with a bottle of painkillers and instructions to have the health aide change his bandages every day.

No one would travel from the village to speak for the shooter at his first court hearing. The judge would decide whether to let the man wait for the trial at home or stay in jail until someone could bail him out. While lawyers at the hearing rattled on about flight risk and community safety in legalized English, the shooter might silently pray that someone would help his school-aged son check the salmon net he had just set in a big eddy downriver from the village.

The judge would set bail and appoint a public defender to represent the shooter. Now relying on a White lawyer who he couldn't understand without the help of a translator, he'd decide to plead guilty rather than let his lawyer call his cousin a liar in front of a jury. Then he wouldn't return home until he had served at least seven years of a ten-year sentence in prison.

Deprived of the man who had always filled the freezer with moose meat and kept them supplied all winter with firewood, his family paid a great price for the shooter's crime. While the State of Alaska kept the shooter fed and warm, his family had to rely on help from other villagers, including the man with a healed bullet hole in his arm. Homesick, the convicted man might look for ways to keep sober when he returned home. Since they didn't provide prisoners with addiction treatment, the man would have to do it on his own.

After his family had caught, butchered, smoked, and dried seven summers of salmon, the shooter would fly home in a mail plane, wearing something other than an orange jumpsuit for the first time since he left the village. He might stay sober for a few days or months, but he would eventually drink and violate his probation. Violating probation almost always led to a return to jail. He, like the criminal justice system, couldn't get traction.

When I reached the village, I walked to the bingo hall, an unpainted plywood building standing above boggy tundra on stubby creosoted blocks. I climbed a set of wooden plank stairs and pulled open the door. The overhead lights were off but I could see long rows of tables and chairs in the light coming through a row of slider windows. A four-by-eight-foot bingo scoreboard hung on the far wall. On bingo nights, the caller sat at the table in front of the sign. He pulled ping pong balls from a blower and shouted out the number painted on each ball. He'd flick a switch that lit up the same number on the sign. During the hearing, I would sit in the caller's chair with the clerk's cassette tape recorder placed on the table, where the blower normally sat.

A handcuffed Mr. Nicolai and his trooper escort walked into the bingo hall after flying in a trooper plane from Bethel. They were followed by an interpreter and Mr. Nicolai's public defender. The defense attorney flew to the village with the district attorney in another charter plane. But they had split up after arriving in Tuluksak so the public defender could speak confidentially with Mr. Nicolai. The trooper took a seat just far enough from Nicolai and his lawyer so he couldn't hear their conversation. People from the village trickled in. Some looked around and then left. Others settled in for the hearing that was scheduled to start in twenty minutes. The D.A. entered and made eye contact with the defense lawyer. Together, they walked outside.

Carol arrived and placed a stack of log sheets, a pen, and some blank cassette tapes on the table next to the recorder. Then, she tucked a gallon-sized freezer bag of dried salmon into the sample case.

Expecting the D.A. to call witnesses, I placed a chair close to the recorder. The lawyers returned and took seats in the front of the makeshift courtroom. They were joined by a group of older Yup'ik men whom Carol identified as members of the village's Traditional Council. The other seats in the bingo hall filled with members of the village.

The lawyers stood and asked that we go on record so that Mr. Nicolai could enter a guilty plea to one count of Criminally Negligent Burning, a misdemeanor. If I agreed to accept the plea, I would have to sentence him. That would be much more stressful than holding the scheduled preliminary hearing to determine whether the state had enough evidence to take Mr. Nicolai to trial. Because Mr. Nicholai had confessed, the hearing wouldn't take long. Since magistrates lack the authority to preside over felony hearings, I could then pass the case off to a superior court judge. If I agreed to accept the plea, I would take final responsibility for the case.

The lawyers wanted me to give Mr. Nicolai a sentence based on the recommendations of the Traditional Council. The D.A. would not ask for Mr. Nicolai to serve any more than the 45 days he had already spent in jail awaiting this hearing.

While the D.A.'s words were translated into Yup'ik, I looked at the defendant and then at the faces of the other people in the makeshift courtroom. They showed no emotion. It was as if Mr. Nicolai had no enemies or friends in the room. In the Lower 48 States, such blank faces would suggest boredom. On the Kuskokwim, I recognized the villagers' reactions as a form of silent respect.

Some judges, including my boss in Fairbanks, would have advised me to reject the D.A.'s proposal. A 45-day sentence for burning down the community hall would normally be seen as too light for such a serious crime. Worse, accepting it would mean yielding the court's authority. I'd be giving it up to leaders raised with a set of cultural laws and expectations as different from the American criminal justice system as those of Japan. Could they fashion a sentence that would satisfy state law? That law required me to impose a sentence on Mr. Nicolai that would encourage him to seek treatment, discourage him from reoffending, and deter other would-be arsonists from striking the match.

Given that he had deprived the impoverished village of a community hall, I could have sent him to jail for a year, which was the maximum sentence for a misdemeanor. Some might believe that such a sentence was necessary to get his attention so that he would not start drinking again when he finished serving his time. They would be wrong. Imposing the maximum jail sentence would not have broken the cycle. It would have just kept the wheels spinning. I accepted the plea deal.

I don't remember if we swore in any of the people who spoke at the sentencing hearing. Threats of prosecution for perjury in a culture where truth is expected were unnecessary. Everyone in the room knew the truth and was raised in a place where it was shocking to lie, even to a policeman trying to send you to jail.

Everyone, including the village clerk who explained that they didn't have enough money to repair the damage from Mr. Nicolai's fire, spoke in Yup'ik, the language of the river. This, more than the racks of drying salmon near the bingo hall, sled dogs dozing outside in the late afternoon sun, or the Asiatic faces of the people assembled in the bingo hall, confirmed my colonialist status.

I assured Mr. Nicolai that he could tell his story at the end of the hearing, then asked if anyone wanted to talk about him or the fire he set. I don't recall anyone speaking out against him. When family members and other people who loved him spoke, they usually had to rub tears from their faces with the palms of their hands.

If the D.A. or public defender made statements, I don't recall them. Since they understood that it was a decision for the Traditional Council, they probably gave up their right to talk. When Mr. Nicolai spoke, it was to tell the village in Yup'ik, that he was sorry.

After having the five council members stated their names for the record, I explained, "Because of the plea agreement, I cannot sentence Mr. Nicolai to jail for more than 45 days. I can order that he pay you restitution, which is money you need to repair the building, but only if he has the ability to pay." After my words were translated into Yup'ik, I said, "I can order him to do community service, like hauling firewood or water for Elders. Since he was drunk when he set the fire, I should order him to undergo an alcohol evaluation and follow any treatment recommendations." I seem to remember at least one of the council members saying "Ii-i," which is Yup'ik for yes, after the last words were repeated in Yup'ik.

Finishing up, I told the council that I could order Mr. Nicolai to pay up to a $5000 fine and to be on probation after he completes any jail sentence. If he breaks his conditions of probation by drinking or breaking the law he would go back to jail and stay there for more than 11 months. "I will enter whatever order you ask for as long as it complies with the law."

Carol turned off the tape recorder. No one spoke for a while. Having a White person's abhorrence of communal silence, it seemed like an hour went by before one of the council members spoke. Since I only had a five-year-old's Yup'ik vocabulary, I couldn't follow their conversation. But I could tell that no one spoke until sure that the previous speaker had finished.

As they conferred, my mind drifted. I wondered if we would be done before it became too dark to fly home. I thought about the king salmon strips that Carol had placed in the court system's sample case. Would it be impolite to ask for one? Could I eat it in front of all these people?

The council president, a man with a face darkened by long hours spent fishing in the strong June sun, cleared his throat and said, in English, that they were ready to talk. Carol turned on the tape recorder. In Yup'ik he said that Mr. Nicolai should get alcohol treatment and do community service to help the village Elders. He didn't have any money, so I shouldn't order him to pay restitution or a fine. He should be placed on probation for five years. If he broke the law again, he should go back to jail.

I didn't tell the council president that I would have fashioned a similar sentence. Mr. Nicolai stood with his public defender, and I imposed a sentence based on the Traditional Council's recommendations. I finished with, "If there is nothing else, the court is adjourned." As if I had given the final amen in a church service, tension left the room. I heard laugher for the first time since we landed in the village. Mr. Nicolai smiled at his family, said "quyana" (thank you) to his lawyer. People waited until Mr. Nicolai left the hall before walking out the door.

Many years after the hearing, his public defender told me that she could find no record that Mr. Nicolai was ever arrested again.

I've seen defendants practically skip out of court after the D.A. reduced their felony charge to a misdemeanor and they received a lighter sentence.

When I was a defense attorney, I often had the impression that the only thing my client cared about was jail time. They didn't worry about how long they would have to be on probation or what would happen if they were caught violating it. Usually nothing happened at their sentencings to trigger the kind of metamorphosis Mr. Nicolai underwent in the Tuluksak bingo hall.

Unlike the typical case, not only were the people of Mr. Nicolai's village present at the hearing, they controlled its outcome. When he said he was sorry, he said it to his victims, not an out-of-town judge. When he was ordered to undergo alcohol treatment, stay sober, and help the village's elderly, he understood that his village would hold him responsible for complying with the order.

Dirty Work

I'm three forkfuls into a silver salmon steak when the phone rings. Must be magistrate business. Only the cops and troopers call me at home. Everyone else just shows up unannounced at the door. In my cautious judge voice, I say hello. The state trooper Harley Davis responds:

"Bud Brown found a body, a floater. What are you going to do about it?"

He's testing or teasing.

After ten years on the Kuskokwim River, I know about teasing and also about the need to maintain a professional detachment when faced with crime or sorrow. That would be the test. In the village I am coroner as well as magistrate, so I ask, "Can you get it with your boat if I help?" He agrees and tells me to meet him ten minutes later at the trooper's float.

I know the compact, gray-haired trooper well enough to call him "Harley." He gets the tough death calls, the ones that involve suicide or an infant's death. When he had phoned from a village and asked me to forgo the autopsy of a baby, I heard sympathy in his voice for the surviving parents. He had watched more than a few cry as their child's body was loaded onto a plane.

But he likes to tease.

The troopers moor their blue-striped aluminum boat to a wooden float anchored to Aniak beach. Harley shows up five minutes late, squashing a mosquito into the fabric of his trooper-blue utility jumpsuit—the kind they use for dirty work.

Harley crosses the float and climbs over a gunwale. On the boat, he pushes a switch that lowers the outboard prop into the river. I stay on the float as he hits another switch to start the motor. The river is as flat as the light on this overcast day. It's warm on the float, but I'll cool off quickly when the boat starts moving unless I sit in its half-enclosed cabin.

The dead guy we're after must be the pilot who crashed his floatplane just downriver from Aniak during the June king salmon season. Without luck, searchers dragged heavy hooks for him through places where current often delivers the dead. He has been in the river long enough to plump with decomposition gases and float ashore. Since no locals had drowned in the river this summer, it must be him. Did he have a family? Someone will have to call them. Now I dread two things.

How bad will he look? I can't guess. A mortician sanitized all the bodies I had ever touched. As coroner, I issued death certificates, granted permission to transport bodies, and ordered autopsies. The sadness of most of those deaths didn't touch me because usually Harley or another law enforcer stood between me and the body. Today, only latex gloves will separate the dead pilot's flesh from mine.

Harley smiles and waves me on board. I untie the boat and swing a leg over a gunwale as the boat drifts away from the float. He smirks. Is he planning to tell people about how close I just came to falling between the float and runabout? I almost trip on a body-sized plastic bag that slides around the smooth deck. He smirks again. Harley takes a seat behind the steering station and pushes the throttle forward. He offers me the other seat but I stand by the motor where there is no chance for conversation. Standing exposed helps me to maintain the numbness I will need to help get the body into the bag.

We pass a man tending a drift net from the back seat of his open skiff. The net forms a deep, porous wall across the current. Some of the white plastic net floats jerk when silver salmon swim gill-deep into the net mesh. The boat driver waves as we pass. Does he know why the magistrate and trooper are in such a hurry? Was his cousin one of the suicides that I processed after taking over the magistrate job?

I take a seat next to Harley, who smiles again and shouts out an offer of coffee. He has already poured a mug for himself from an almost-new thermos. *Is he trying to discomfort me with his apparent lack of concern? Is he testing or teasing?* He knows about the criminal defense work I did in Bethel before taking the magistrate job. Then, I was another pesky lawyer helping criminals avoid responsibility by poking holes in trooper cases. Now, I can issue search warrants, order him to arrest dangerous criminals, and require him to transport a body for autopsy. I should expect testing and teasing.

Harley will retire soon. After a law enforcement career in the Fairbanks-Wasilla-Anchorage rail belt, he transferred to Aniak for his last three years of service. It's a trick the old troopers use to ramp up their monthly pension checks. The State of Alaska pays troopers more money per hour for working in the bush. Harvey receives a higher paycheck now and can expect inflated pension payments after he retires. Later, when my hair is as gray as his, I will concede that a career spent helping victims of crime and loss justified such payback.

Harley slows the boat and shouts over the droning engine. "It floated up there, on that gravel bar just below Bud's salmon-drying racks."

I spot something man-sized and indistinct as driftwood resting just out of the water. Harley throttles back so the boat wake won't rock the body when he turns to land. The pilot's gas-bloated corpse distends his sweatshirt and jeans. Harley unrolls the body bag next to the pilot and pulls down an industrial grade zipper that bisects the bag. As I pretend that this is as normal as a fishing trip, Harley lifts the wallet and a comb from the rear pockets of the pilot's jeans. He slides them into plastic evidence bags.

The trooper carefully tucks one zippered edge of the body bag under the pilot. Taking up station on my side of the body, he tells me to kneel next to its legs and slide my hands under the thighs:

"When I start to roll it onto the bag you do the same. Be careful. He's been in the water all summer and we don't want an arm or a leg to fall off."

I hide my fear, tell myself that collecting the dead is one of the village magistrate's responsibilities and that I should be grateful that the troopers usually do it for me.

Now close to the body, I finally smell the sweet but rotten scent of spoiled meat. It is not as foul as decayed salmon or a moose carcass. But I know I will never forget it.

Someday, I will wonder why I did not vomit or run away. Did Harley expect that? I want it over, but work with as much care as the trooper to make sure we bag an intact corpse. I remember that the pilot has a wife down in Texas. I'll have to call when we get back to the village. For her and for Harley, I carefully lift the body into the bag.

The pilot's swollen face is the last to disappear as the trooper zips up the body bag. I will always be surprised that the hair, while coated in river silt, still looked alive, that the river had turned his skin the color of the mahogany wood I used for carving, that it had relaxed his features into a calm expression.

There is no graceful way to lift a full body bag over a three-foot-high gunwale and lower it onto a boat deck. The trooper and I try our best. Someday I would appreciate the consideration he showed the body. I will realize that he asked for my help because no other trooper was around to help him. He did use the retrieval to tease me. Eventually I will accept that at the end of a career that required him to deliver the worst news, and investigate those who hurt others, he was entitled to use gallows humor to tease a former defense attorney.

I sit in the passenger seat on the way back to Aniak. Harley is all business, no talk, as he maneuvers the boat alongside the trooper float. Since the body doesn't belong to a village family, no one waits for us on the beach. I stand on the float while the trooper drives his truck down to where we can transfer the body into its bed. He hands me the clear evidence bags and I stare at the pilot's black comb as Harley drives me to my office. If he hurries, he has time to slip the pilot into a coffin-shaped tin box and ship it to Anchorage on the evening flight.

When the sound of the Anchorage jet takeoff fades, I call the widow in Texas. I should have called her an hour ago but stalled, trying to think of how to break the news. For the other village deaths, Harley or another police officer notified the next of kin. Will the pilot's wife faint, scream, or blubber? I should be prepared for tears, maybe hysterical sobbing. Will my voice crack with emotion? Good thing Harley left.

The phone rings as I realize, in a panic, that it is the middle of the night in Texas. She answers before I can hang up. With the voice of a young woman who cannot sleep, she says, "Hello."

Today, I cannot remember her name so I call her Mrs. Stevens. I respond to her greeting with, "Mrs. Stevens, this is Dan Branch, the Aniak magistrate."

"Yes."

For some reason I open the bag holding the dead man's comb. Its smell of decay floats up as I say, "I am afraid I have some bad news."

"You found him."

"Yes."

"Thank God!"

"Mrs. Stevens, I am afraid that he is dead."

"I know. I didn't think he could still be alive. But now I can tell the kids. We have a body to bury. The insurance will pay. Thank you."

"We weren't able to recover any salvageable personal effects. There is a comb and a wallet but you probably won't want them."

If she asks me to send them to her, I will have to tell her that they smell of death. She doesn't want them, just the body. I warn her about the required autopsy and promise to issue orders for the eventual shipment of her husband to Texas.

The smell of the wallet and comb waft up every time I open the coroner file drawer. Long after I leave the river, I remember that smell and how hard it was to wash it from my hands. I will not forget the sense of relief I felt after that call to Texas.

The Fire Extinguisher

Infatuation with an Alaskan nurse drew a young doctor named Lars away from his ordered life in Sweden to bush Alaska. The nurse, Darcy, had met the doctor the previous winter at a Swedish medical conference where his superior knowledge of local language, culture, and landscape had defined their budding relationship. Calm in a place that could not surprise him, Lars had charmed. During a series of expensive long-distance phone conversations, they had planned his summer visit to Darcy's home in Bethel. He arrived with a war surplus rifle, a wilderness survival kit, and a set of thirty-year-old topographical maps of the Kuskokwim River.

In Bethel, Lars had to accept Darcy's superior knowledge of all things local. He had to struggle with the village's primitive sewer and water system, his new role as a member of a racial minority in Yup'ik country, and the lack of decent coffee shops.

Several days after he had deplaned at the Bethel airport, Lars helped load Darcy's sixteen-foot river skiff with gear and the twenty-four gallons of boat gas needed to reach Aniak, one hundred and thirty miles upriver. Lars, who had never driven a river skiff, couldn't object when Darcy grabbed the tiller of her thirty-five-horse motor and nosed into the Kuskokwim current. He sat in the middle seat, where he served as ballast. Referring often to the maps in his lap, Lars shouted out directions. Darcy ignored what little of the advice she could hear over the outboard. She knew from experience that the river had altered its course many times since the publication of the maps.

Fear of sloughs gripped Lars on the trip. He yelled, "No, Darcy!" every time she pointed the skiff into a shortcut provided by one of the side channels. Perhaps Lars's English-Swedish dictionary defined "slough" as a branch of the River Styx. Ignoring Lars's misleading directions, often shouted in a pedantic voice while she steered her fast-moving skiff around sand bars or partially submerged logs, wore on Darcy. It turned the trip upriver from Bethel into a living hell instead of the romantic ride she had planned with Lars during the previous winter's phone calls. She didn't recognize the bossy man in her boat who showed so little trust in her navigational skills.

An hour before sunset on a clear and warm August day, I left the log house that Susan and I shared in Aniak near the village jail and drove our yellow Yamaha three-wheeled ATV onto the thirty-foot high dike. The gravel and dirt barrier surrounded Aniak like an earthen fortification to keep water and river ice out of the village during the annual spring floods. My trailer bounced behind the ATV on the dike trail, its slat sides rattling when it hit one of the many potholes.

I stopped where I could see a fish wheel secured to a mid-current gravel bar downriver from the village. Its two opposing wooden and hardware-wire baskets rotated in and out of the river on a wooden axle. The push of current on the submerged basket forced the other one forward until it too dipped into the water. Late afternoon light flashed on a silver-bright salmon lifted from the river by a rising basket. Just below the wheel, a sixteen-foot metal skiff moved upriver carrying a hunched-over man waving his arms about while the woman driving the boat looked away. Darcy and Lars had arrived.

Darcy, who said she needed to stretch her legs, walked to our cabin. Lars agreed to ride back with me on the ATV. A clean-shaven, six-foot-tall guy with blue eyes and brown hair, he dressed like a foreigner with some local knowledge: yet-to-be-washed Carhartt canvas pants (a bush

Alaska gold standard), hi-tech Swedish raincoat, and waterproof cap with earflaps. Lars watched me, a slump-shouldered guy who smelled of insect repellant and fish slime, load the trailer. I sported department store jeans (frayed cuffs, legs black from grease, fish slime, and soot), one of the "Aniak Halfbreeds" sweatshirts that the high school kids sold to raise money, and a new "Markair" ball cap that I had saved for this special occasion.

Lars slid behind me on the ATV's banana-shaped seat and we bounced home the long way. Darcy and Susan were drinking tea when we walked into our cabin. Darcy's face was already fading from windburn red to a healthy cream color. We ate Louisiana-style blackened silver salmon with Chinese cabbage from our garden and Susan's pie for dessert. Lars had little appetite for the salmon. The next morning, we loaded my 16-foot Starcraft skiff for a trip to the archeological dig site at Kwigiumpainuka-miut (Kwig Dig) to show Lars some more of the river and visit friends who worked at the site.

Susan and I were always looking for a way to pay Swedes back for how they saved her life. After we fell in love, Susan moved to Biskops Arnö Folkhögskolan near Stockholm to study documentary photography for a year. That winter she was diagnosed with Non-Hodgkin's Lymphoma. I was visiting her in Sweden at the time. One of the surgeons told me that she only had a 10 percent chance of surviving. He was wrong. With radiation and chemotherapy, cancer doctors at the Uppsala University Hospital cured her.

Swedish friends had taken care of Susan as she recovered from the chemotherapy. Her Swedish foster parents had served us lutefisk with potatoes and white sauce on Christmas Eve. The goodwill I felt for Sweden and its people because of the kindness showed to Susan made me want to treat this Swedish doctor to a special sampling of Kuskokwim life. But Lar's passive response to everything we showed him during his visit made it hard to keep the grumpy man from pouting.

As we loaded my skiff for the Kwig dig trip, silver salmon hovered in the lee of fish-cleaning rafts that were anchored just off the beach. Through a hole in the center of the raft, the owners had dropped netted silvers into a submerged wire cage. The imprisoned salmon attracted rainbow trout and Dolly Varden char. A village kid fishing with a willow stick, string, and a twenty-five-cent hook pulled out game fish larger than Lars had ever seen in his home waters. He started to assemble his high-end graphite fishing rod until I stopped him. On the Aniak beach, adults never competed with the kids for trout or dollies.

After stowing the gear, including the padded case containing Lars's rifle, I slid all but the skiff's bow into the river and boarded. Hershey, our chocolate-brown water spaniel, followed. Lars and Darcy, again friends after twelve hours on dry land, took the middle seat. Susan tossed in the anchor, pushed the skiff into the river, and sat in front. The current grabbed and pushed us down river until I slipped the old Evinrude twenty-five-horse outboard into gear and pointed the bow into the current. Even with its heavy load, the skiff rose up on step as if lifted by strong hands and skimmed over flat water toward the Yup'ik village of Chuathbaluk.

Hershey leaned on Susan in the front seat and pointed his nose upriver. Wind created by the skiff's passage pinned back his long, curl-coated ears. Lars stared at the white spruce forest that lined the eastern bank, broken only by thinly spaced cabins and Mr. Nelson's homespun sawmill. I watched the river ahead for drift logs, looking sometimes at the willow thickets that lined the western shore. The Russian Mountains rose above the willows like giant eroded molars.

Chuathbaluk, Alaska, *Summer, 1987*

Ten miles upriver we passed Chuathbaluk, where low bush blue-berries hung ripe on the southern slopes of the Russians. Susan, Darcy, and I might have been picking blues if we weren't entertaining Lars. The Swede seemed relaxed on the ride to the dig. He never took out his maps and only gestured once with his hand and that to point out a grey wolf trotting along the beach above Chuathbaluk. I didn't stop or slow down so he could photograph the animal. The noise of the Evinrude prevented me from telling Lars that wild things on the river take cover when a skiff drops off step.

As the Kilbuk Mountains started to reduce our view of blue sky, I beached the boat near the campsite of Mary, an archeologist, and her art-ist-helper, Terry. They were working on excavating Kwigiumpainukamiut, an old village site.

The women lived in a large tent set up between the beach and bumpy terrain dotted with birch trees. The ruins of a sod house hid inside each bump. Mary promised to show us her excavations the next morning.

Between the boat and Mary's tent, a line of brown bear tracks led through the most promising place to set up our tents. Each paw's five spear-like claws pointed upriver. Mary told us not to worry. The grizzly hadn't been around for a week. After studying the bear's tracks for a few more seconds, she advised us, with a little laugh in her voice, not to keep food in our tents.

Susan and I set up our tent far away from the bear trail. Darcy and Lars put theirs on the other side of a low rise from it. We all returned to the beach and built a driftwood fire for cooking. Lars, who had not smiled since he saw the bear tracks, watched the Alaskans roast Polish sausages on thin willow spears. We talked, paying more attention to sto-ries than our sausages, which charred before we rescued them. Lars used the heat reflecting off a careful arrangement of rocks to give his meat a golden-brown glow.

Sunset was still a couple of hours away when Lars left for his tent. I started telling river stories. The sound of a rifle shot interrupted one about a brown bear mystery. On the river, gunshots didn't raise worry unless grouped in threes—the universal signal for distress. After the shot's echo died, I continued.

Darcy went to check on Lars. In minutes she returned.

"He's OK. His gun went off when he was cleaning it. He will come back after he finishes sewing up a hole in the tent."

After Lars rejoined us, we roasted marshmallows. Only our Swedish friend's had the liquefied center and tan exterior of a gourmet roast. Ours caught fire thanks to inattention, but we ate the blackened sugar without complaint. As the fire burned out, Lars said, "Everything you eat is black." Believing this to be a good-natured rebuke, we all laughed, ignoring the sour look on his face.

The next morning Darcy looked rested but not Lars. Since neither complained about mosquito bites, something else must have interfered with his sleep. He did seem pleased to see the cheese, cucumber, and homemade Swedish-style bread that Susan set out for the morning's frukost. I enjoyed my open-faced sandwich on a slice of bread that I had burned while trying to toast it over the fire.

After breakfast, Terry showed us the beautiful pencil sketches that she had made of a pair of grass socks. Mary said that they had last been worn over a hundred years ago. They looked like they could still warm feet inside sealskin boots. A few years before our visit to the Kwig Dig, grass had saved a man near Bethel. During a sixty-below blizzard, he had avoided hypothermia and frostbite by stuffing dried grass between his skin and soaked clothing after his snowmachine sank into an open lead of the river.

Lars showed little interest in Terry or Mary's work. After mid-morning coffee, we said goodbye and headed downstream to Aniak. We planned to stock up on camp food in the village, refill empty gas tanks, and leave the next morning for a fishing trip up the Aniak River. On the way home we would fish a slough forty miles up from the village that an old homesteader claimed was full of trout.

Because the twenty-five horse pushed us downriver at a good pace, I shrugged off my worry about how the old outboard seemed to struggle the day before after I changed gas cans just above Chuathbaluk. Lars looked over my shoulder at the skiff's wake spreading out in an expanding "V." If he was excited about the trip up the Aniak or frightened of what might happen up there, I could not tell. Maybe he was as tired of my company as I was of his. After he shot his tent, nothing I did or said seemed to interest him.

Lars could have felt fear. They have brown bears in remote parts of Sweden but Lars had never seen them or their tracks. Back home, he had never compared his prints to the ones left by a bear like he had at the Kwig dig. He might have relaxed if his guide demonstrated care, confidence, and skill. But, he was stuck with a local careless enough to let his food burn. He might have also resented the physician-like control I exercised over the boat like Darcy had held on their ride up from Bethel.

Lars's eyes flared when I cowboyed the skiff around a partially sunken spruce log that I spotted just before ramming it. We all had to hold on when the skiff rolled onto its port gunwale after I threw the tiller hard over. I hadn't driven the skiff onto a gravel bar yet but the near misstep must have eliminated any remaining confidence Lars had in my boating skills.

A marine layer of clouds hung over Aniak while we loaded the skiff the next morning. As I found a place for his rifle, Lars tried to assure me that, "The Swedish military had trained me in the safe use of that weapon." The words worried, rather than comforted me. Anyone could fire a rifle. The trick was to know when not to do it.

I never carried a long gun, like Lars's rifle, that could kill at distance. I didn't want to be tempted by fear to fire at a curious bear that meant no harm. I didn't want to face the fury of a wounded animal. Had the Swedish army training taught him such restraint?

The skiff strained to climb on step as we headed up the Kuskokwim to the mouth of the Aniak River. I blamed the extra gear and gas we carried. We turned into the stronger current of the Aniak River and crept by the Swede's Place—the old blond's homestead now used by a newcomer to raise lettuce and New Zealand White rabbits. I maximized the gas flow and steered the skiff toward a cut bank where the faster current had gouged out a deep path through the river bottom. A large, "C" shaped gravel bar reached into the river from the opposite shore. The cut bank and gravel bar changed places at the next bend. I could avoid grounding the skiff by steering it from cut to cut.

Twenty miles upriver, we closed on Brown Slough. I smiled every time I motored the skiff past the slough because we had anchored our skiff in a slough of the name when we still lived in Bethel. Debris pushed into the Aniak by the Slough had formed an irregularly shaped, mid-stream gravel bar that was hard to read. My first trip up the river, I had bounced my stainless steel prop onto the gravel bar several times before watching an Aniak neighbor cross it using an invisible channel. After that I had waited at each tricky point of the river until someone taught me by example how to navigate the hazard.

The current picked up after we passed Brown Slough. The skiff no longer out-ran the mosquitoes that flew into the boat when we passed near shore. It took three hours instead of the usual one to reach the Fish and Game salmon counting weir. We waved at the college students who tended it. Our slow speed allowed me to study the twin of my twenty-five-horse Evinrude outboard that lay on the beach in front of their camp.

The river became braided. Sections of swampy birch forests displaced the white spruce woods that had dominated the downriver area. The outboard died while we rounded a bend. Veterans of my successful past adventures that had been made interesting by equipment breakdowns, forgotten gear, or a wrong turn, Susan and Darcy calmly watched the skiff drift downriver until trapped in the circular current of an eddy. The current carried it to a gravel bar where Susan hopped out and buried the flukes of our anchor into the gravel. Hershey, our dog with chocolate-colored fur, and even darker brown eyes, joined her, followed by Lars and Darcy. When Lars spotted large brown bear tracks mixed among the giant goat-like tracks of a moose, he slid his rifle out of its case and reached for some bullets. After chambering a round, he reminded me again that he had been trained by the military in Sweden to operate it.

Wanting coffee and a chance to think through the outboard motor problem, I started up our battered Coleman camp stove. After he patrolled the gravel bar, Lars watched me pump air into the stove's gas tank. If worried by the tank's chipped paint or the rust on the generator tube that fed aerated fuel into the stove burners, he did not say. Mosquitoes descended on us as we drank our afternoon coffee, so we quickly finished and jumped into the boat. Susan and Darcy sat in the front seat. Lars took the middle one after returning the rifle to its case. Hershey huddled at my feet.

Guessing that I had a fuel problem, I removed the engine cowling and used a quarter to loosen the screw that held in place a wire-mesh filter screen. Gas drained into the shallow well formed by the inch-high wall of the metal engine frame to which the cowling attached. I felt smug when I found several flecks of red paint stuck to the mesh screen.

I cleaned the screen, set it in place and hand-tightened the screw that secured it as mosquitoes crawled into my ears and eyes. After quickly clamping the cowling back on the motor, I squeezed a rubber bulb in the fuel line to replace the gas that had leaked out when I cleaned the screen. The engine sputtered but did not start, so I squeezed the bulb several more times. When it still didn't start, I squeezed repeatedly for a long time. In a few minutes I would learn that I had not securely tightened the fuel filter screw. I would realize that raw gas had filled up the engine casing. Everyone in the boat would hear the explosion of gas vapor trapped inside the cowling. They would see the cowling fly into the air and watch me fish it out of the eddy. They would notice that flames encircled the engine block. I asked Darcy whether she brought her fire extinguisher.

"Yes. Lars, give this to Dan."

Lars squinted at a gauge on the white cylinder.

"Darcy, did you inspect this fire extinguisher before the trip? I think it has been discharged."

Lars held on to the extinguisher while he argued with Darcy. Yellow and orange flames leaped up the blue engine block. Black smoke rose from the flames as they melted the rubber coating on the engine's electrical wires. The never-brave water spaniel whimpered at my feet. I grabbed a five-gallon bucket full of camp supplies, emptied it out, filled it with river water and doused the flames. That ended the threat of immolation but left us with oars as the only way to move the skiff.

Lars slipped his wallet into a sealable plastic bag, secured it in his waterproof duffle, and said, "Don't panic. I have been trained by the Swedish army in wilderness survival technique." Without asking, he seated the oars and took the rower's position. It was the wallet-into-the-bag maneuver, which conveyed his utter lack of faith in my abilities to guide us home, that finally got me. I wanted to kill him or leave him on the gravel bar where the mosquitoes could do the job.

Okay, he didn't know that I had towed a four-cord raft of firewood logs down this channel last fall when low water increased the number of places to ground the skiff. He hadn't spotted my motor's twin resting on the beach near the Fish and Game weir. He didn't know that our landlord had loaned the students the motor and they were probably trying to figure out a way to send it home.

Lars came from a country where the forests had long since lost mystery and its people expected fulfillment, not adventure in the woods. The yellow cross on Sweden's sky blue flag could stand for safety. Swedes rarely poisoned themselves with wild mushrooms. A prudent Swedish outdoorsman would never enter the mouth of a wild, bear-infested river until a qualified mechanic had certified the integrity of his boat and motor.

To demonstrate my lack of concern, I cast for salmon and trout as the seven-mile-an-hour current carried us downriver. Susan and Darcy pulled up their parka hoods against a suddenly intense rainstorm. Lars used the oars to ease the skiff away from sweepers and followed my hand signals to avoid gravel bars. I thought about taking over the oars when we approached the logjam. That barrier of uprooted spruce trees would have blocked the whole river if someone from the village hadn't chain sawed a skiff-sized gap through the jam last spring. We needed to line up the axis of the skiff with the center of the gap and hold that line or the current would slam us sideways into the driftwood wall. Then we would flip or sink. Lars lined us up and we slipped through, surfing the arc of white water that poured through the gap.

After a decade living where conflict avoidance is a cultural mandate, I wanted to end the tension between Lars and myself after the skiff passed through the logjam gap. This meant allowing him to think that he had saved us. It meant admitting, if only to myself, that things could have gone very, very wrong. That should not have been difficult. When we lived on the river, things were often close to going very, very wrong. If we wanted to get mail during the thin ice times of spring or fall, we walked across weak ice carrying a canoe paddle to pull ourselves out of the water if we fell through. When we needed firewood or wanted fresh fish in the winter, I drove our old snowmachine upriver, even when the temperature hung at 40 below zero. If the snowmachine motor flooded I'd scrape carbon off the sparkplug and tip the machine on its side so gas could drain out of the sparkplug hole. It never occurred to me to stay home. If he lived in the village, Lars would never chance thin ice or leave town on a cranky snowmachine. Near avoidance of something going very, very wrong was a new experience for him.

I decided to ignore the tension and Lars as much as possible. The river widened after the logjam and offered no more obstacles until we reached the Fish and Game weir. Lars followed my directions and beached the skiff near the surplus twenty-five-horse Evinrude.

The weir tenders came out of their canvas wall tent to greet us. One was female and the faces of the males were covered with "I forgot my razor" beards. All were excited to see us. Maybe they spotted the home-made cookies that Susan held in her hand.

We sat on rocks around a fire circle, a tea mug in one hand and a cookie in the other. Hershey, who once ate most of a chocolate birthday cake, turned his begging eyes on me as I started on my second cookie.

After hearing our motor-on-fire story, one of the students offered us the use of my landlord's outboard. In minutes we lifted off the fire-damaged Evinrude and replaced it with the working one. It came to life after a few pulls of the starter rope. Lars, Darcy, Susan, and I took seats in the boat. It was harder to convince Hershey to leave the friendly camp, where he hoped to filch from the weir tenders' dinner. With the borrowed motor, we lifted up on step and rode the current toward Aniak. In minutes we reached a mud-bottomed back channel that opened into a small pond. The homesteader who lived three miles up the Kuskokwim River and thirty-five miles from here claimed the pond was a very productive trout hole. A thick wall of inward leaning willows prevented any land access.

Dog salmon, their dull silver bodies already tattooed with blood-red and slime-green spawning stripes, rolled on the pond's surface. I cut the motor, and asked Lars, who sat in the front seat, to drop the anchor. Susan and Darcy assembled their spin casting rods as Lars flicked a lure in the direction of the nearest dog salmon. He had a strike before I could free my rod case from the big fish box that held our food and gear.

It rained as we fished. A low cloud ceiling worked with the willow barrier to turn the pond into a claustrophobic cell. No wind reached us to discourage the mosquitoes that acted like we were their only chance to feed before winter. We doused ourselves with DEET but it only discouraged a few wimps. I kept losing lures by letting them sink to the bottom as I swatted or scratched. Lars, acting like clean living had made him immune to the mosquitoes' bites, hastened the death of several terminal dog salmon. No one hooked a trout. Realizing that I was the target of another of the Kusko homesteader's jokes reignited my anger. He must have known that it was a good hole for mosquitoes, not trout. I secured my fishing rod and looked for the first time at Susan and Darcy. Army-green mosquito netting covered their heads. They had replaced their fishing rods with knitting needles that clicked variegated Swedish yarn into watch caps.

Lars agreed to pull in the anchor but couldn't resist one more cast as I started the motor. He hooked another dog salmon, which he towed behind the skiff as we returned to the river.

As we droned down the river, I thought about Napaimute, an old gold mining town ten miles upriver from the Kwig Dig, now diminished to one house and a dock. The house, a white two-story with sash windows, sat back from the river on a low hill. Before it was disassembled for moving from a failing upriver gold town—Flat or maybe Iditarod—a person with a good hand had painted a number on every one of the tongue and groove boards that formed the walls. This simplified its reassembly at Napaimute. It was rare on the river to lavish such care on a building. People were more likely to build new or drag their old homes with them on spruce pole sleds. A house had to be well loved to justify the care shown the Napaimute home. In a remote land with harsh weather, people could not afford to love a building. I regret that I didn't take Lars to Napaimute so he could have had coffee in the much-loved house. It would have given him an hour or two in a place of comfort during a visit when he was always on edge.

Lars sponged down the skiff after we unloaded it on the Aniak Beach. *What would the guys down at The Lodge say about this?* I wondered as the Swedish doctor washed away dog salmon slime and blood. Those guys, hunkered over coffee and a burger plate if they had the cash, spent their energy feeding their families and keeping them warm. To them a clean boat must signal a weak salmon run, a busted motor, or a fisherman too broke to buy boat gas. It meant failure.

They grew up learning how to avoid the mistakes I made. Yup'ik elders taught them how to maintain an outboard motor and find open river channels before they hit their first gravel bar. I came to the river ignorant but lucky. After buying a skiff, I had learned from my many mistakes and by watching the skilled locals. But, whenever an upriver bound moose hunter rounded a corner eighty miles up the Aniak and saw me driving toward him, I always saw surprise and sometimes a little fear on his face.

Lars had a map on his lap the next day when he and Darcy left Aniak. Susan and I watched from the beach. Before Darcy's skiff reached the downriver fishwheel, Lars shot his arm out like a policeman directing traffic. Susan said, "Let's hope she doesn't kill him before they reach Bethel."

Blind Faith

No one thought to take a picture of the four brown bears that moved with purpose towards our camp on an Aniak River gravel bar. Susan was one of the campers and good friends with the other two. At a recent dinner, they confirmed that there were four bears, one for each of us. The number is significant because we had only one gun—my Winchester 12-gauge shotgun, and it only held three shells. I wondered whether to send all three into the mother, or use one or two on her nearly grown cubs. Any one of the bears could have killed us.

We shouldn't have been on the river during dog-salmon time when over a hundred thousand of the big fish were making their one-way passage to the spawning redds. The chance to fatten up for the winter on rich fish flesh drew brown and black bears to the river. We had floated for days over sex-mad salmon in our inflatable raft. When we stopped for coffee on a gravel bar, spawned-out fish swam close to our feet as if asking for a quick death. Their long trip through fresh water had robbed them of their sleek, chrome-sided ocean beauty and left them with garish red and green striped sides and hooked jaws. A scattering of dead monsters decorated almost every beach. Clouds of their decay hung in the air.

The first night of the trip we camped on a wide gravel bar abutting the edge of a tundra plain that spread west for over a hundred miles to the Bering Sea. With no trees in sight, we couldn't hang our food, so we crammed it into 5-gallon plastic buckets with tight-fitting lids and carried them a hundred feet away from our tents. The next morning, we found the buckets still full and the track of a bear that had circumnavigated our tents. With my boot, I measured the tracks and determined that the bear would require at least a quadruple-wide size 14 shoe.

After breaking camp, we paddled down a narrow canyon with twenty-foot-high gravel walls. Entering the broader Aniak River at lunchtime, we steered the raft over to a graveled peninsula and secured it to a tangle of driftwood logs. Susan and I walked to where the peninsula bordered a white spruce forest and found a deep pool warming in the day's sunshine.

We ate a lunch of hard cheese and Swedish Knekkebrød (unleavened rye bread), then stripped and jumped into the pool. The falsetto scream I released after hitting the cold water made Susan laugh. It also startled a very large brown bear that was watching us from twenty feet away. The bear froze for a moment as if to confirm this people sighting, then disappeared into the white spruce forest.

Eight other brown bears watched us float downriver that afternoon. When not eying us, they worked the shallow channels between gravel bars, grabbing salmon from the water with their mouths or slapping them ashore with a front paw. None made a move on our raft full of food and flesh.

Late in the afternoon we entered a section where the river ran deep and fast between steep-sided gravel bars. We landed on one in the middle of the river and decided to camp on it after a search produced neither dead salmon nor bear tracks. A bear would starve before it could catch a salmon in the swift water near the bar so we figured we were safe for the night. From our campsite we could look across a fifty-foot-wide channel to open tundra blood red with lingonberries.

While I fired up our battered Coleman gas stove, a large brown bear sow and three yearling cubs, each almost her size, walked across the tundra and slipped into the river. They rode the current diagonally across the channel and washed up at the bottom end of our gravel bar, two hundred feet away. The sow sniffed the gravel where we had walked during our bear track search and then squinted at us. We banged pots and yelled, "Go away, bears." They moved closer. The raft sat between the bears and us so we ran down the gravel bar and carried it behind our camp. Mama and her teenagers quickened their pace.

As Susan and the others repacked the raft, I slipped my shotgun out of its case. It only took a few seconds to load with a slug and two double ought shells so I had a lot of time to watch the bears approach. They didn't charge, just ambled towards us, stopping every ten or twenty feet to sniff the air and stare. Still damp from their river crossing, their blond guard hairs glowed in the late afternoon sunlight. I didn't want to kill or even wound such beautiful things, and I didn't want anyone in the boat to die.

With little hope of solving the problem with what was loaded in the gun, I slid a hand into my jacket pocket and found a shell filled with number five shot that I had brought along in case we spotted a tasty duck. The shell's tiny pellets would only annoy the bears but the noise might scare them off, so I chambered it and fired the gun over their heads.

The sow rose on her hind legs in one fluid motion until she stood taller than an NBA forward and then dropped into a run. Her children followed her into the river. They crossed the channel and climbed a cutbank to the tundra. Without looking back, the grizzlies ran in the direction of the Bering Sea—four shrinking beings glistening in the low-angled light.

Crap. Why hadn't I rushed everyone into the raft and let the bears have the run of our abandoned camp? That would have been the smart move. Why did I hold the ground, with the mother of my future child and our close friends behind me, with so little skill with a shotgun, and with no chance of knocking four bears down with three shells? Even though the bears swaggered toward us like self-assured street thugs, I could not believe we were in danger. I had faith in the bears and my luck—perhaps too much faith.

We re-launched the raft and paddled downriver until darkness required us to pull out on another gravel bar. One of us tended a large bonfire all that night. I read by firelight coming through our tent wall from the fire. When tired of my book, I slid down into my sleeping bag. I didn't glow with the self-admiration of a hero, didn't thank God for deliverance or the Winchester factory for the twelve-gauge. A Fourth of July firework would have worked as well for running off the bears. I reran the memory of the sow standing like a transfigured saint, her wet fur aglow in the late afternoon light. Thanks to the duck shot, she and her children had been more afraid of me than I had been of them. Crap.

Inertia

When I checked the mail on a July Monday morning in 1988, a white business-sized envelope was hiding among the other mail jamming the courthouse post office box. At first glance, it looked identical to the other white envelopes in the box. Those contained copies of court orders or memos from the Bethel or Fairbanks courts.

After emptying the post office box, I carried the mail to the aluminum-sided trailer that housed the Aniak courthouse and jail. Since it was Monday, I had to empty the honey bucket before putting the kettle on to boil or reading the mail. The bucket was full with human waste deposited by jail guards and prisoners over the weekend.

I was very interested in opening the white business-sized envelope after I read the return address. It was from the Office of the Attorney General. Before that Monday morning, I had tossed AG job announcements in the woodstove after glancing at them. The prestigious Attorney General's Office would never hire a self-taught guy like me, who had only practiced law in the bush, to handle the complex litigation that made up their caseloads. But the envelope I opened contained notice of an opening for a child protection attorney in Ketchikan. I'd done a lot of that work as a lawyer in Bethel. The Bethel superior court judge often appointed me to serve as a master on child protection cases involving Aniak families. It was the first time an AG job notice stirred me to action.

There was much I'd miss if we moved from Aniak where we lived on a salmon-rich river near tundra, mountains, and white spruce forests. My job isolated us from the community, but deepened my relationship with Susan. We supplemented the marginal fare from the store with fish from the river and food grown in our garden. It was a pretty good life until Susan volunteered to help out at Grandma Mary's daycare.

Before we moved to the village, Susan had worked as an early childhood specialist in Bethel. A state education commissioner that Susan impressed when we lived in Bethel had told Grandma Mary's Day Care to ask her for help. Susan volunteered to show the day care staff ways to encourage kids through games, craft projects, and reading.

Susan found the kids watching cartoons on a television when she walked into the day care on her first visit. She spent to rest of the day observing. After the kids headed home, Susan asked the day care workers to share ideas on how to help the kids. They had some great ones, including ways to help the kids become better readers.

Over several weeks the children and staff enjoyed changes and suggestions to their routine. Apparently Grandma Mary was not pleased and complained to the day care board. At their next board meeting, without providing a reason for it, they asked Susan to resign from her unpaid job. We talked about leaving the village the next day.

Things at the magistrate office were soon to change for me. In a few months, the court system was planning to increase my pay grade and order me to work from 8 A.M. until 4:30 P.M in the courthouse. This wouldn't been justified by an increased caseload in Aniak, but by the larger number of cases that I would need to cover in Bethel because the D.A. wouldn't let the Bethel magistrate handle them.

The pending plan to turn my magistrate job into a full-time position made me think for the first time of leaving Yup'ik country. While in Bethel, I had turned down offers of jobs in Anchorage. No one had offered me such a route out of the bush after we moved to Aniak. Susan and I had become comfortable objects at rest. Grandma Mary brought us to inertia's tipping point.

I drafted a legal resume on my old Kaypro II computer, listing the dates of my undergraduate degree from U.C. Berkeley and my Juris Doctorate from the University of San Francisco. I added a description of my five years working in a Bethel legal aid office and five more years in private practice. To get their attention, I mentioned how many jury trials, coroner inquests, and child abuse hearings I had conducted while a magistrate.

Resume restrictions didn't allow me to describe the challenges of representing a caseload of clients spread out over an area the size of Kansas who were more comfortable speaking Yup'ik than English.

There was no place on the state's standard job application for listing the skills acquired by an attorney practicing law on the river: patience, willingness to honor Yup'ik cultural rules, the ability to shrug off or at even bury the horror from reading police reports and medical records of abused children. Those were the skills that I had acquired while other candidates for the Ketchikan job were likely drafting contracts and questioning witnesses at depositions. I sent in the completed resume and application to Juneau with little hope of being offered the job or even an interview.

A month later, a secretary from the Attorney General's Office in Juneau called to schedule a telephonic interview. I was pleasantly surprised but not optimistic about anything coming from it. They had probably wanted to interview me so they could check a box on their way to hiring the preferred candidate from a high-end Anchorage law firm.

After we arrived in Aniak, Susan and I had signed up to receive TV shows from a village cable company, including all the Chicago Cubs games. While waiting for the AG office interview to begin, I lay on the couch with our spaniel, Hershey, on my stomach, watching the Cubs play on cable TV. When the phone rang, I muted the television before answering. Lack of expectations kept me relaxed as I answered their questions about trial experience and how I had organized my one-person law office in Bethel. I wanted them to know that I had had a heavy law practice in Bethel before we moved to Aniak.

When Hershey barked, I thought they'd quickly end the interview. Instead, they extended it with questions about the spaniel and about the sled dog team I had recently disbanded. That evening, over dinner, I warned Susan not to expect much. A month later, the supervising attorney for the Child Protection Section in Juneau called to let me know that the Attorney General wanted me to take the child protection job in Ketchikan. It took another four months for her to get final approval from the Governor's office. During that time, we learned that Susan was pregnant. That gave Susan a good reason for accepting my long pending marriage proposal. We would wed in Aniak, before leaving the bush for Ketchikan.

A few days before Christmas, 1988, I flew from Aniak over to the Yukon Village of Holy Cross to perform a marriage service for an Atha-baskan couple in the bride's home. Snow was forecast, the kind of storm that grounds planes for a week. But I agreed to go, wanting to end my magistrate career in Aniak with a marriage rather than a coroner's inquest.

After the mother of the bride pushed play on a portable cassette player, a Buffy Sainte-Marie song filled her little government-built house. The bride, wearing a white dress that showed her baby bump, made her procession down the hall of her childhood home and into the living room. I had to smile. In a few days, Susan, whose baby bump was barely noticeable, would marry me in Aniak. The Holy Cross bride approached me like I was her high school principal at graduation. The groom stood by my side, still wearing a ball cap. After asking the bride's mom to lower the volume on the cassette player, I read from a marriage service script that I had copied from the state magistrate manual. Five minutes later, they were man and wife. They kissed. I shook their hands. The groom left, having never taken off his hat. I walked through the snow to the Holy Cross airstrip.

Fat snowflakes partially obscured the Aniak runway when the Holy Cross plane landed. But the storm soon ended. The next day, sunlight brightened our last Christmas in Aniak, which was spent packing for the move to Ketchikan. The next day our wedding guests arrived.

Friends flew into the village from Bethel and Sitka. The next morning, December 27, 1988, I phoned around to invite people in the village to the Catholic Church for the wedding. We thought the late notice would give them an excuse for not giving us gifts. But the missionary gave us a box of towels and the homesteaders across the river gave us a box of tanned rabbit skins.

Susan walked up the aisle wearing a black corduroy jumper and clogs as "Joy After Sorrow" played over the church public address system. My shirt was periwinkle, tie lavender, clogs black. After Father Andy pronounced us husband and wife, we ate the angel food cake that Susan had baked the night before and returned to our packing.

Another snow storm charged in from the Bering Sea that afternoon to close the Aniak Airport. With no way to return to their homes, the out-of-town guests spent our wedding night in our bedroom. Three slept on the floor and a fourth shared our bed. We all remained chaste in our individual sleeping bags.

The next day, our guests escaped Aniak on the only plane that managed to take off. Susan and I watched it disappear into the snow and wondered if we would be so lucky the next day.

Just after noon on December 30, we rode in a friend's pickup truck to the airport. Snow fell on my old Kay Pro computer, bicycle, and Hershey's kennel in the pickup bed. After carrying our gear and two suitcases into the air cargo bay, we placed everything on a wooden pallet and took seats in the waiting room. Ten other ticketed passengers were already there, including a school teacher from an upriver village and his family. They had already waited three days for a flight out of their village. Yesterday, during the weather break that allowed our friends to leave, they had escaped to Aniak. They just missed the flight that carried away our friends.

We spent four hours drinking airport coffee, reading, and rubbing Hershey's wavy fur. Every half hour the school teacher's wife demanded an update on flights.

Everyone in the waiting room stood up when a Piper Navajo rattled out of the snow. The pilot, a friend of mine from Bethel, walked into the waiting room, spotted Susan and me and waved us over. We followed him into the cargo bay, where we could talk without being heard by the other passengers.

Looking like a musher trying to unload an ornery lead dog, he said, "I saw your names in the passenger's manifest. Are you ready to go?"

Puzzled, I answered, "Yes."

After he asked if we had much gear to haul, I pointed to the dog and the stuff on the air freight pallet.

Smiling, he said, "Follow me."

We did. While we walked out the plane, a cargo guy loaded our stuff into the plane's cargo hold. The pilot asked me to take the copilot seat.

Susan and Hershey sat in the back. After telling me to put the co-pilot headset on, he started up the engines. Before he could taxi to the runway, the wife of the school teacher appeared out of the snow and started pounding on the pilot's door. She screamed "Take us with you. You can't leave without us."

The pilot shut down the engines, cracked open his door and told the woman that another plane was coming to take everyone to Bethel in time for the evening flight to Anchorage. He cut off further conversation by closing his door. The woman retreated to the waiting room as we taxied onto the runway. When we reached the end, he turned the plane around and said "it looks like a mile visibility to me," and opened both throttles. Before I could respond, we were airborne.

Ten minutes after taking off, the Navajo burst out of the clouds. I had to squint against the sunshine bouncing off the snow-covered tundra below us. If we had gained a few more thousand feet in elevation we could have seen all the way to the Bering Sea. Now that he could multitask and I was no longer convinced that we would crash into Mt. Hamilton, I asked him why he left the school teacher and her family behind. He said that the storm was lifting and the airlines was really going to send a plane to get them to Bethel in time to board the evening jet to Anchorage.

Before I could ask him why he asked us to board, he handed me a stack of court documents and asked me to explain how divorce court worked.

PART THREE

Southeast

Someday I'll Miss This Place Too

Through breaks in Ketchikan rain
I can almost see the Kuskokwim River
twelve hundred miles away.

A convoy of snowmachines moves up river from Kalskag.
Empty fuel drums rattle in the drivers' homemade sleds.
They wave.
The river community is too small
not to wave.

Now home in a rainforest town,
I kayak deep-water fjords but miss driving
a string of dogs out of Aniak at sunset,
miss seeing the pups' long moon shadows,
miss how they pulled toward the Buckstock River.

In my truck, parked near a drive-through window,
I eat French fries instead of the jerked moose meat
I had washed down with dense tea as the sled dogs rested.

Ignoring shouted Happy Meal orders, I slip back to Aniak
where village church bells ring the hour

as relatives drag the river for Bummy's body
remember that life in the village
was not as joyful as a sled dog's meal
or as simple as their panting rhythm.

I banish thoughts of village deaths
and fill the void with a sub-arctic sky darkening
from blue to purple to a black field for stars.

When rain obscures the Kuskokwim,
I watch Ketchikan eagles fight
over tourist-tossed French fries,
accept that I'll move again. Kindness
in this Southern Alaska town is burnishing
my memories of the Tongass
so someday I will miss this place too.

Following Raven

The students, all Tribal members, spaced themselves at long, flat tables. Some had already picked out a chopping block from a pile of red cedar rounds near the door. Each had their own adzes—double-beveled steel blades, maybe 1/2 by 4 inches, lashed to wooden handles with braided-nylon cord called halibut gangion. I'd heard about adzes but not seen one before.

After 12 years living in the Yup'ik country of southwest Alaska, I was comfortable with having the whitest face in a room. When I lived on the Kuskokwim River in Bethel, Yup'ik people helped rather than hindered my efforts to catch salmon that might have fed their families. But the students assembled for Dempsey Bob's carving class were not Yup'ik. They belonged to the Tlingit, Haida, or Tsimshian tribes of Alaska's Southeast panhandle region. Carved totem poles illustrated their clan stories, which could not be told in word or wood without their clan leaders' permission. Would my fellow students be as welcoming as the Yup'ik people?

I took a seat next to a kind looking man with an adze and set of traditional north-west-coast knives. The knives all had a three-eighth-inch

Close-up of Raven head spoon

wide steel blade attached with gangion to a short wooden handle. After learning that he was a Tsimshian named Ken, Wolf Clan, and that he was born and raised in Ketchikan, I asked him to name his knives.

"The ones with a U-shaped bend are crooked knives. This one with a shallow curve is a not-so-crooked knife. That one with no curve is a straight knife."

My tools, a set of hobby chisels, remained hidden in a plastic grocery store bag. Some had shafts with shallow bends but they weren't not-so-crooked knives. Nothing in my shopping bag could scoop out wood like a crooked knife. I worried that when the teacher saw my tools, he'd toss me out for being unprepared.

My cheap knives would have stayed in a box of other "in case there is time" things if not for my friend, Tom. During the social hour at my church, he said he was going to take a carving class at the Totem Heritage Center, taught by a Tlingit master carver from Prince Rupert, B.C. named Dempsey Bob. The students would learn how to carve a grease spoon. Since the Totem Heritage Center was funded to help Native elders pass on carving skills to their young people, I asked how a non-Native like him got into the class. Tom said the classes were open to everyone. He assured me that the center had made him feel welcome when he'd taken a tool making class the previous year. I would be OK as long as I didn't act like a tourist. Planning to use Tom as a security blanket, I signed up for the class without having ever seen a grease spoon.

Tom hadn't arrived at class by the time Dempsey Bob walked into the room. He looked over his students with raptor-intense eyes split by a hawkish nose. I might have left right then if I hadn't had another motive beyond learning to carve a grease spoon. I needed a positive place to spend time with Tribal people in Ketchikan. Having worked for just two months as a child protection attorney in the District Attorney's Office, I was already starting to measure the local Tribal community by my caseload. After years of defending juvenile delinquents and representing parents in child protection hearings in Bethel, I now prosecuted them. Without the personal interaction I would have had with the kids or their parents as their attorney, they were becoming two-dimensional villains.

Cases involving crimes or child abuse in one of the nearby floating timber camps didn't skew my feelings about the White people that lived there. My dad had been a logger and miner in Montana. Some of our Rocky Mountain family still worked in the woods or in the Potlatch pulp mill in Lewiston, Idaho. I had assumed that most of the men cutting down the old growth trees on Prince of Wales Island had the taciturn dignity of Cousin Cleve; their families the same capacity for love and kindness as my Aunt Anna.

Without the Heritage Center, I saw no possibility of having Native friends in Ketchikan willing to shared tea and stories like we had in Bethel. In that Kuskokwim town of 3,000, even though I was always an outsider, I sang with a Yup'ik church choir, was teased by Yup'ik co-workers, and learned from an elder how to catch king salmon in a drift net. My wife, Susan and I were welcomed minorities. I regained majority status in Ketchikan, where I didn't have any counterbalancing experiences with Tlingit, Haida, or Tsimshian families. Susan and I had mostly socialized with cops, social workers, and the people in the D.A. office. I hoped that the Heritage Center classes could offer me a bridge to the local Tribal communities.

I had first tried woodcarving in Aniak during the spring thaw, after a dam of broken ice formed on the Kuskokwim River. The resulting flood shut down the village power plant and turned our lot into an island. Trapped and without the diversion of television or stereo, I pulled a chunk of birch from the woodpile and attacked it with a set of cabinetmaker chisels that I used for making dog sleds.

Time passed without notice as the wooden mallet smacked a chisel's handle, sending chucks of birch to the floor. From the tiny speaker of a battery operated radio tuned into a Jesuit-run radio station broadcasting from Nome, rock music gave way to the sound of nuns chanting the rosary, Father's thought of the day, the Tundra Telegraph ("To Mary in White Mountain, your order at the A.C. Store is in"), then more rock music. I stopped directing the mallet, let the chisel align itself. I fancied that an unseen hand moved the chisel, like Dr. Zhivago's pen in his frozen Siberian greenhouse, until the carving's crudeness shattered the illusion. In Dempsey Bob's class, I was like the guy enrolled in a language program who hoped his English skills would form a platform for learning Mandarin.

Tom walked into the classroom fifteen minutes after Mr. Bob and set out the tools he had made in last year's class. No one reacted to his late arrival.

We followed Mr. Bob outside to find a pile of alder rounds. He told us that they came from a ninety-foot high tree that my table neighbor Ken had cut down that morning. Ken's alder was just leafing out so the rounds were heavy with sap and smelled like spring growth. At Mr. Bob's direction, each student searched for a round of alder with straight grain and few knots. As we sorted through the pile, Mr. Bob told us that Tlingits carve eating utensils out of alder because it does not transfer any flavors to the food. I managed to find a round, eight inches across, without any obvious knots. I split it in half with a maul and kept the half-round with the straightest grain.

The master carver drew a line on a chalkboard that mimicked the smooth dip and rise of an ocean swell. Pointing to the drawing, he said, "Tlingit carvers try to capture wave forms in their grease spoons." He sketched in the deep curve of the ladle and a handle shaped like the stylized head of a wolf. Looking at the drawing, he told us how grease spoons were used to welcome visitors from another clan.

"Fat was scarce and valuable in those days. When a different clan's canoe approached, the local leaders would meet the paddlers on the beach with a grease spoon filled with oil from Hooligan, also called candlefish. The head of the visiting clan would drink until the spoon was empty of grease. Today, for ceremonies, we use tomato juice."

He told us to adze the back of our alder half-round until perfectly flat and then draw a pencil line down its center. "If you don't have an adze," he said looking at me, "use one of the ones in this box." I watched Ken use his adze to level out the back of his alder round then copied his actions without question. Surprised at how long it took to square up the wood, I chopped away until Mr. Bob told us to clean up so we could go home.

Returning the next evening, I took my alder half-round from a plastic garbage bag, still just a piece of firewood with a flat side. Ken used a carpenter square to draw a line down the center of his alder and lines on the top and bottom of it that ran perpendicular to its now flattened back. I did the same. Dempsey Bob told us to draw parallel lines 2.5 inches on either side of the center line then adze away all the wood on the outside of them. The uncoordinated sounds of twenty men adzing with various levels of skill filled the room. The dull thuds of sharp steel striking wet wood blended as more and more adzes struck at the same time. Without willing it, my adze took up the uniform beat. Later, in a class taught by Reggie Davidson, a Haida carver from the Queen Charlotte Islands of B.C., I would adze to the beat of the teacher's skin drum while he sang songs learned from his grandmother.

During the class, Ken talked to me about making tools and the Seattle Seahawks football team with their northwest coast style logo of an osprey. He explained that his daughter was without a clan because children inherit clan membership from the mother and his ex-wife was a non-Native.

Knowing Ken's clan membership, Dempsey Bob drew a wolf figure on the handle of his spoon. Looking at my tools, he suggested that I not try to carve an animal crest on mine. Before class, Tom had told me that non-Natives needed special permission to use totem figures, like the wolf or frog, but that it was OK to carve an eagle or raven. Thinking he was enforcing cultural property rules rather than making a realistic estimate of my skills, I told Mr. Bob that I'd like to try to carve a raven on my spoon. "We'll see," he said before moving down the table.

Lee Wallace, Haida, Brown Bear Clan, arrived late on the second night of class. While loosening his tool roll, he told Ken that his wife had just delivered their second child, a girl. My daughter and Lee's youngest would later play together and Lee's oldest daughter would be her babysitter. The men teased Lee but then congratulated him. He quickly caught up and passed most of the students in the class, his adze as precise as a band saw blade.

Like a master playing twenty chess games at once, Mr. Bob moved from student to student, giving each his next move. Lee had reduced his alder to a sharp-sided 5-inch by 14-inch block by the time of the master's visit to his workstation. Mr. Bob drew the outline for one half of a grease spoon on the back of Lee's block, handed it to him and said, "Do the same on the other side, then take everything away from the outside of the lines. Use a saw to cut stops where the bowl starts to curve out." I stopped adzing to listen to Mr. Bob's instructions to Lee, then handed him my wood.

Rather than draw a spoon outline on my block, Dempsey Bob handed it back with instructions to, "bring this down so it's flush with the line. Same here." This happened at least twice as I reduced the width of my block from 6 to 5 inches. On the third or fourth visitation, he drew on the line marking the outside of the spoon and handed the block back to me. He only gave what I needed to complete each step. None of the other students received more.

I was learning as an apprentice learns the carving trade. Watch, listen, be quiet or you won't get it. Progress in small steps; complete each to near perfection before moving on. Maintain symmetry at all costs. Keep your tools sharp, your pencils well pointed, your mouth shut unless you can sing the traditional songs or tell a good story.

No one sang in that class but we heard good stories and some teasing. Ken and some of the other students accused me of carving a duck decoy rather than a grease spoon. No one cursed or shared a lewd joke. Every good story met with affirmation from the students. I relaxed in the resulting atmosphere of trust, watched how other students complied with Mr. Bob's terse instructions, accepted without question his order to, "Do it again, better this time," or, "Now do the same on the other side."

I learned to hold the wood in my left hand while carving with a tool in my right. At the end of the first week of classes, my carving almost resembled a spoon. After I had scooped out the inside of the ladle and brought some symmetry to the outside of it, I handed it Mr. Bob. He peered down the centerline, checked that each side of the handle had a smooth, flat surface, and said, "Raven?" After I nodded a yes, he drew the outline of a raven's beak and forehead on one side of the handle and said, "Do the same on the other side, then carve away everything above the line."

When I had first asked Mr. Bob to let me carve a raven on my grease spoon, I wanted an image that would remind me of the fun-loving ravens that had entertained us in Bethel. After the other birds fled south, ravens flew through winter skies, performing purposeless acrobatics, flips and dips, in temperatures well below zero. They would work in teams of two to steal food from our sled dogs. One would pluck hair from the back of a feeding dog then fly a few feet away. While the dog went after his tormentor, the other raven snatched kibble from the dog's bowl.

During a class break, I found the image of a more suitable raven outside the Totem Heritage Center. He stood atop a totem pole that told the story of his marriage to Fog Woman. Created by master carver Nathan Jackson, Fog Woman's Raven stood erect with eyes canted downward like a proud but cautious sovereign. I returned to my carving tools, and hoped that Mr. Bob would help me carve an effigy of this impressive raven on my spoon.

Later I was to learn that Raven, in a time of darkness, tricked an old shaman to free the stars, the moon, and the sun from the old man's bentwood boxes. He also watched the first man emerge into the world from a clamshell. In the years after the grease spoon class ended, Raven was to remind me of the depth and beauty of Ketchikan's Native culture at times when my work only revealed ugly things.

By the time I started carving Raven onto the spoon, bandages covered all my fingers, one for every slip of a chisel. The other students teased me about my frequent use of the center's first aid kit but said kind things about the spoon trying to escape its alder prison.

Each evening the spoon lightened as I removed more wood. I focused on completing tiny assignments from the master carver, trying to copy what he had done while I watched. Near the end of the two-week class, he reduced the raven's eye to a raised column, and then in the next step rounded it into a dome before carving in the eyelid form. I tried the same on the other side. Many Northwest Coast artists form raven eyes with the same abstract shapes used to represent the eyes of other totemic creatures. The ones I formed on my spoon under Dempsey Bob's guidance mimicked the penetrating, mildly cynical stare of the breathing bird. When both eyes looked right to Mr. Bob, he showed me how to make the shallow-crescent nostril slits that pierced both sides of the beak.

On the last evening of the class, wondering how I would finish the spoon on my own, I carried it to Dempsey Bob for the next lesson. Squinting, he sighted down the beak, turned it this way and that, then handed it back to me saying, "At some point, you have to stop carving and call it done." Free to move beyond the apprentice's narrow view of the spoon, I saw all of it for the first time—the deep swelling bowl with symmetry confirmed by the alder's growth lines, the simple, strong raven head, the spoon's arching curves mimicking a raven in flight.

"Fly," I whispered as I cradled it in both hands, half expecting it to lift away. "Nice spoon," said Ken, as he packed up his tools.

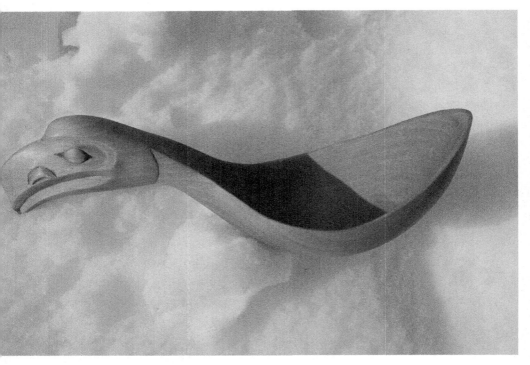

Raven head spoon

The Last Seat

An old white guy in knit cap and Walls insulated overalls slept next to the last open seat on the Alaska Ferry *LeConte*. Quietly taking the seat so as to not wake him, I smelled fuel oil and hard drinker's sweat. The crew had turned off the lights so I could see our reflection in one of the lounge windows–two gray-haired men with laugh lines deepening into wrinkles around the eyes and the corners of our mouths.

Over the intercom, the *LeConte's* purser announced the ship's 7:00 a.m. departure for Haines and Skagway. My neighbor slept though the announcement and the ferry's exit from Juneau's Auke Bay Terminal.

I envied his ability to sleep through the noise and wondered why his face didn't show more evidence of hard drinking. To help me ignore his smell and the chattering din of the other passengers, I skimmed a *Smithsonian Magazine* for photographs of the arctic or other empty spaces. My neighbor woke when I slipped the magazine into the dark space beneath my seat. In the assured voice of a storyteller, but with that near-Minnesotan accent of Bush Alaska, he said, "Must be a good read."

"Yeah."

Reaching under the seat for the magazine, I asked if he wanted it.

"No. I'm getting off soon in Haines. Been down in Juneau to stock up on those peaches that Costco sells in glass jars. Filled the car with them."

He explained that he wanted to get back to his place along the Haines Highway before the spring construction season. After partying the previous night, he had overslept and almost missed the boat.

He shared his opinions of Juneau (too big, unfriendly and crowded) and Haines (too much politics for a little town). I told him that I understood how he could find Juneau unfriendly but that most of its people were actually nice. Fear of commitment inhibits them from smiling at anyone but their friends. They worry that one smile given to a stranger would require them to smile at that person every time they met. Rather than show any teeth, they remain strangers because their stressful lives do not have space for even one additional relationship, no matter how shallow. He replied that in Haines everyone had to smile or at least say "hi" when they passed someone on the street. The town was too small to let people think you were better than they were. He smiled at people even if they teased him about his dog, which had died six years ago. They gave him a hard time because he had built a concrete mausoleum for the animal. His girlfriend had given him the pooch when they had lived together in Anchorage.

"I keep the path to her crypt cleared of snow all winter, so I can visit her in the morning. People think I'm nuts to spend so much time and money on a dead dog, but I don't care. Came from Aniak, like the girlfriend."

I gathered that the dog had stuck but the girl hadn't. And saw, like sun breaking through fog, the connection I didn't know I was looking for. My magistrate job in Aniak had separated me from people in a village where, like on the crowded ferry, I was as exposed as an aquarium fish. In Aniak, I'd felt as though everyone judged me, the judge, even my choice of dogs. After Susan and I had imported a curly-coated Water Spaniel to the village for bird hunting, Susan overheard someone at her work whisper, "The magistrate has a poodle."

Looking around the *LeConte*, I wondered if the expensively dressed cross-country skiers that filled the other seats scrutinized me as they apparently had my smelly neighbor when they left open his adjacent seat. Finding no hint of judgment on his pale face, I said, "I used to live in Aniak. Maybe I knew her. What was her name?"

"The dog's name was Susie."

"No, the girlfriend."

He told me her name. I had never met the woman when I lived in Aniak, but I had helped a man from Napaimute Village with the same last name check on the safety of his daughter in Anchorage, so I asked whether the daughter was his old girlfriend. In a voice that revealed surprise and what might have been jealousy, he asked, "How well did you know her?"

"Didn't, but I knew an old trapper named Mori, who was her father. He once came down to my magistrate office to talked to me about her."

After his pursed lips relaxed into a smile, he said, "Oh, yeah, he was a character. I think I'll head back and get something to eat from the cafeteria."

Twenty years before the ferry ride to Haines, Susan and I had lived in a poorly insulated slab shack on the northern bank of Aniak Slough. In winter we could walk across the frozen slough to the village. When it was ice-free, we crossed the half-mile wide slough in a canoe. During freeze-up, in November, pans of ice on the slough made the crossing dangerous. While I considered navigating a path around the ice on a Saturday so I could visit the village post office, someone knocked on the door. I opened it to find an old man with small Asian eyes, pale skin, and flat features on a round face. He stood maybe five foot three and wore heavy insulated overalls—the kind used by snowmachine drivers in cold weather. A tipped-back hat made of three marten pelts rested on his head. Over his overalls, he had fastened a worn leather harness to hold the stump of his right arm tight to his body. He told me his name was Mori and that he had come down river from Napaimute that morning in a skiff.

Mori asked if I was the magistrate. When I admitted that I was, he asked me to help find his daughter. He hadn't been able to reach her the day before using the one phone in the village of Chuathbaluk.

I knew the man by reputation. The son of a Yup'ik mother and a Norwegian Sámi brought to the Kuskokwim River by the Federal Government to herd reindeer, he lived with his elderly wife in a cabin about twenty miles upriver from Chuathbaluk Village. Everyone on the river said he was tough. I'd thought he was a myth until he stood at the top of my cabin steps, wet with melted snow.

I asked him in for tea, but he said he didn't have time. He was worried that the ice islands now floating downriver would soon jam. If that happened, he'd be stuck in Aniak until the ice firmed up enough for snow-machine travel. I agreed to call his daughter using the courthouse phone. People in need commonly asked me to make phone calls for them. The confidence in their face when they asked for help told me it was considered part of the job; made me realize I had assumed the responsibility to serve as well as punish when I had donned judicial robes. Having served for five years in the Bethel Legal Services Office before moving to Aniak, I didn't mind helping people. It was much harder to send them to jail or banish them from their families after an act of domestic violence.

In the village, I made few friends because I feared I would not be able to rule fairly in cases where friendship for the victim or the defendant might cloud my judgment. I worried that neither would find a court order fair if they thought my affection for a member of one of their extended families influenced the outcome of the case. Magistrates serving larger communities rarely sat in judgment of a friend or neighbor. But in Aniak, I sentenced the postmaster and the trash collector my first week on the job. Later, I arraigned a man on an assault charge just minutes after he had fixed the courthouse plumbing. I saw no choice but to serve the village in isolation. Had I erected an unnecessary barrier between the village and myself? Could I have lingered on a bench seat at the Aniak Lodge, drinking coffee with guys I might have to sentence the next month?

That snowy Saturday the worried father powered us through slough ice to Aniak in his old flat bottom skiff. He shopped at the Alaska Commercial Store while I checked the mail. Then we went over to the courthouse. The previous night must have been quiet because no one was sleeping off a drunk in one of the courthouse jail cells. I called the phone number he gave me. When a man answered, I told him I was the magistrate in Aniak and that his girlfriend's father hadn't heard from her for a while.

In a guarded voice, the kind people use to answer cop questions, he said, "She's fine now. We got into a fight, and she took off for a week or so. Now she's back, sleeping it off." He spoke without drunken slurs or the half-whisper favored by the hung over.

The father didn't want to talk to his daughter's boyfriend so I hung up after asking him to let the woman know about the call. As he looked down at the courthouse's filthy floor, the father said, "She's still drinking. That's bad. Can you stop her?" Not sure if other magistrates had been able to solve his past domestic problems, I told him there was nothing I could do.

"We worry about her. She's got a kid, you know. She can't take care of the kid when she's drinking." The next summer I learned that his granddaughter stayed with him each summer. Mori had come into my magistrate office for help to get rid of a brown bear that was taking fish from his smoke house.

In an effort to make him feel a little better, I told him that his daughter's boyfriend sounded like an OK guy. He said, "He's OK, but he drinks too. Not so much. Doesn't get so crazy when he parties." I thought that she could have a worse roommate but didn't say anything more to the man.

Now that my own adult daughter had moved far away, I could understand why a father navigated around ice islands for thirty miles to check on his girl. But on that day, I just worried that I had not given him the help he needed.

All that was twenty-some years ago. Was the guy who'd left for the cafeteria the same one I talked to on the phone that November Saturday?

Thirty miles south of Haines, the *LeConte* pulled past the eight-sided lighthouse on Eldred Rock. I thought, as I usually did on a ferry run from Juneau to Haines, of the ideal life a guy could live isolated on the tiny island. White, with crisp lines and a widow-walked tower rising above the slanted roof like a Russian Orthodox Church dome, the lighthouse promised an ordered, simple life for its keeper. On a rock that discouraged visitors, I could sit alone and look at the mountains of granite and glacier rising up both sides of Lynn Canal. It'd be quiet enough to hear humpback whales surface and sea lions growl. No one would be able to see enough to judge my actions. After a few months, the island's silent solitude might become oppressive, but I longed for it as we passed the lighthouse on that crowded ferry.

Away from the main snowmachine trails through Aniak, we'd had silence most days in our cabin, but I always assumed we were under constant surveillance, that we lived in a glass bunker rather than a comforting

Eldred Rock Lighthouse, Lynn Canal

hermitage. This seemed fair. I couldn't sentence others for their criminal violations unless they believed that I obeyed all laws—state, federal, and cultural. I tried to act as if Sister Anna Marie, my mean-spirited first grade teacher, kept us under a twenty-four-hour watch.

I wondered if Mori had built his cabin twenty miles from the nearest village for the solitude it offered or for the nearby eddy where he anchored his salmon-catching fish wheel. When my smelly neighbor returned from the *LeConte's* cafeteria, I asked if he had ever visited the old man's cabin.

"Never made it out there, but he and his wife stayed with us when they came to Anchorage."

"What happened to your old girlfriend?"

"Not sure. Her drinking got worse so we broke up. I heard her kid moved out to Aniak to stay with the old man. That was a while ago before I moved down to Haines."

The Haines man and I talked the rest of the passage about peaches, the Kuskokwim, birch trees, and dogs. I didn't ask him whether he was the guy I'd called at the old man's request. I decided he probably was. Even if he wasn't the guy on the phone, he had been part of the Mori's family for a time. That, in the way that only makes sense in rural Alaska, made him part of Aniak's extended family. My job as magistrate made me no more than a shirttail cousin to that family.

The old peach eater and I wouldn't smile at each other if we bumped shopping carts at Howsers' IGA in Haines or Juneau's Costco. But on the *LeConte*, I missed him after he disembarked. His presence on that ferry ride to Haines had freshened my Aniak memories. His words renewed the image of one-armed Mori so wet from dripping snow, his face tense with worry. They dropped me into the old man's open skiff as it plowed through new ice on Aniak Slough. Those memories carried me to the village's spruce and birch forests, then to shared tea and stories at the table of our few Aniak friends. His Bush-accented stories reminded me of Aniak's kind Yup'ik residents. They made wonder what I might have gained if I hadn't sat in a judge's chair.

The Body of Christ

On a subzero Tuesday morning, the cathedral rector pulled on the heavy green vestments of ordinary time. His planned liturgy would echo in a near empty church. But, the four inches of new snow then covering Anchorage roads wouldn't keep away former governor Wally Hickel, nor his wife Ermalee.

Every time I attended morning Mass at the cathedral, the former Alaskan governor and his wife took the same pew near the front. Hickel's profile was as familiar to Alaskans as Lincoln's. I had never met him but knew from newspaper stories that he was an easy man for me to hate.

Two Yup'ik men, ragged and drunk hugged themselves and stamped their feet on the cathedral steps as the priest unlocked the front doors. The priest must have smelled booze on their breath and the fouler scent of the alcohol they had sweated into their clothes. They huddled in the vestibule when I passed through it on my way to the pews. Even in their reduced state, they reminded me of the men I had admired when I had lived in the Yup'ik country of Western Alaska—men from a culture of non-confrontation trained to harvest from the land without destroying its wildness.

I had flown to Anchorage from Juneau the previous night, re-reading the appellate brief I would have to defend before the Alaska Supreme Court a few hours after the end of morning Mass. I needed the familiar liturgy, the forgiveness of sins, the stories, the remembering of the Sacrifice, and the intimacy of the Eucharist. Together, they strengthened my faith and shrunk the scope of my morning's work to something I could handle.

Alone, the green-clad priest processed up the center aisle. Without accompaniment he soloed a song written by popular Catholic writer Bob Hurd. Always the last to find my place in the songbook, I joined in at the second verse. During the penitential rite, the two Yup'ik men took seats in the back pew. One slept. The other looked like he might when watching a boring movie on TV. Both remained quiet until the Consecration when the priest raised high the oversized wafer. Echoing the priest's words, a suddenly engaged Yup'ik man shouted, "The Body of Christ." Shaking his friend awake, he said, "Look, it's the Body of Christ."

Like the twenty other people scattered around the church, I turned to look at the two Yup'ik men. The silent one appeared confused and uncomfortable. His friend smiled and repeated, "The Body of Christ." His face glowed like a holy card saint, inner light emphasizing the confusion of red, busted capillaries on his swollen nostrils. We all turned back to the priest as he genuflected before the newly arrived Body of Christ and said, "Do this in remembrance of Me."

I felt embarrassment for the two men, the kind you might experience when a beloved uncle passes out at your sister's wedding. Their Bush accents and Asian-like faces reminded me of the place where I began my adult life. The men probably grew up on the Yukon-Kuskokwim Delta of Western Alaska where I had lived for twelve years. We had leaned into the same delta winds. They might have harvested pond ice for the drinking water it could provide their grandmother and helped their dad pull salmon from the family set net. I probably drove my dog team over the snowmachine trails they had used on shopping trips to Bethel. If I met them after Mass at the church where I now take communion in Juneau, I'd feel homesick.

We all sang the Great Amen and stood for the Our Father. The inspired Yup'ik man hopped up and dragged his friend from his seat. We all heard the two men chant, "Our Father, Who art in heaven, hallowed be thy Name..." They didn't stumble on the words and I wondered how many times they had stood in their childhood church to say the universal Christian prayer. Today, distant in time from St. Theresa's Church in Bethel where I had prayed the Our Father in English and Yup'ik, I realize how saying that prayer, even in English, could have connected them to their home village, if not to me and the rest of the congregation.

No one shook the Yup'ik men's hands after the priest directed us to offer each other a sign of peace. They knelt during the second elevation of the Eucharist and admitted, with the rest of us, "Lord, I am not worthy that you should enter under my roof but only say the word and my soul shall be healed."

One of the Yup'ik men joined the communion line, head down, hands clasped together at his waist. After each step, he heard the priest tell the person at the head of the line, "This is the Body of Christ." I reached the priest before the Yup'ik man, bowed my head to the Host in confirmation of the priest's exclamation and let him place a wafer in my hand. It dissolved in my mouth as I returned to my pew to pray.

When the intoxicated man stood before him with hands forming a table for the Host, the priest pressed the Body of Christ against his vestments. The Yup'ik man swayed side to side as he said, "I want the Body of Christ. Give me the Body of Christ. I need the Body of Christ." After the request became a chant, the priest dropped the host into the chalice, covered it with one hand and swayed back and forth at each demand for communion. They both believed in the power of the transformed wafer. But the priest's conscience prevented him from allowing his God to enter the man's shaking body—a temple defiled by alcohol.

Unable to feel the calm that normally flows through me after communion, a calm I needed to get through the rest of the morning, I wanted the priest to quiet the man by giving him communion.

Governor Hickel approached the priest and supplicant. In his tailored camel hair overcoat and carefully combed silver hair, he couldn't have looked more different than the disheveled homeless man. When governor, he had sent fear throughout Juneau with threats to cut the state jobs that fueled the town's economy. He had ordered bulldozers to cut a road through Alaskan wilderness in violation of Federal law. I expected him to give the Yup'ik man one loud command and back it up with a threat to call the police if he didn't leave the church.

The ex-governor shook the Yup'ik man's hand like he did the hands of those around him when exchanging signs of peace. I couldn't hear what they said to each other, but after a brief conversation the Yup'ik man smiled, gave the governor a slight bow and returned to his pew at the back of the church.

I understood why the priest withheld the Body of Christ. But, now, after hundreds more liturgies, I believe that the presence in the Host that eventually calmed me and temporarily filled the governor with grace could have helped the Yup'ik man defeat his addiction and return to his home parish. I could only hope that another priest is willing to satisfy his hunger for the Body of Christ.

My Father's Son

Before the Second World War, my father killed deer and elk with a Winchester 30-30. After his discharge from the Army, he gave it to my Uncle Sherwood. All the men and women in the family used it to take their first deer. When my cousin figured out that I was his only adult relative who hadn't shot a deer, he brought me the gun. We both assumed that Dad would have wanted me to kill with it.

The 27-foot Seasport crunches through skim ice as it eases out of its Juneau harbor slip. It's late November. The sun isn't up. We expect five hours of daylight for hunting after we reach Admiralty Island. I sit on one of the boat's plush seats with my father's 30-30 Winchester rifle between my knees. At home, my daughter, dressed for school, walks past the mask I carved of her father's father.

The other friends, dressed in layers, talk about their families, work, or other subjects unrelated to the day's purpose. I wedge the Winchester into a safe corner of the boat, wipe off the gun oil it left on my hands and drink coffee with a man I'll call Bill—the guy I fish with for salmon—a man who knows the obligation attached to the rifle. We understand that this break in autumn storms is my last chance to take a deer with it before the season closes in December.

Winchester manufactured Dad's rifle in 1907, long after its first lever-action 30-30 had "won the West" from the original occupants. I found it a thing of wonder, light but a sweet shot. I could carry it through the old growth forests all day. I was not tempted to rush but rather move with the observant caution needed for a successful hunt.

The gun helped Dad's family survive the Great Depression after his father lost their grocery store in the Montana Rockies by offering credit to those unable to pay their debts. Dad had to drop out of school to hunt and work in the woods while his brother Sherwood rode the rails between migrant farm worker camps. Sherwood sent his earnings home to Montana. Dad used the 30-30 to bring home deer and elk meat.

Bill and I look out through the Seasport's windscreen as the boat bounces into heavy chop at the end of Gastineau Channel. The chop grows into three-foot-high waves where Taku Inlet joins Stephens Passage. Up inlet, the Taku Glacier snakes thirty-six miles from the Juneau Icefield to tidewater. In summer, strong runs of king and silver salmon move through the inlet and into the Taku River to spawn. On this late November day, only confused currents run beneath the Seasport. The boat driver steers into the waves and throttles back until the Seasport no longer slams. We pass steep-sided Grant Island and move toward a sandy beach on Admiralty's Glass Peninsula.

❋

I wanted the Winchester the first time I saw it at my Uncle Sherwood's house on the Washington-Idaho border. In a voice that crushed any hope that the rifle would ever be mine, Dad told me he had given it to his brother after the war. He explained how in 1945, after four years of service in North Africa and Italy, he had taken the rifle on an elk hunt with the old trapper who had given it to him. A bull offered itself to Dad but he didn't take the shot. When the trapper watched the elk walk away, he yelled, "Why didn't you kill it?" Dad answered, "I wasn't sure my bullet wouldn't kill you." Many times, when we were alone, I had asked Dad to repeat the story. Each time I silently rooted for him to take the shot and drop the elk. He never delivered the happy ending.

After Dad died, I found photographs he had taken while stationed in North Africa and Italy. Some of the glossy black and whites show Arab refugee women with eyes deadened, perhaps by witnessing too much loss. One shows a troop transport ship sunk by planes that my father had repaired. I also found a program for the March 31, 1945, performance of Verdi's Otello at Naples' Real Tratro di Carlo. My dad had autographed the program cover, as did the five other American soldiers who sat with him. Until now, I had never connected these things to the gun. I was shocked that my father, who after dropping out of high school and worked as a Montana miner before the war, found such joy attending Italian operas.

The boat driver kills the engine and releases the anchor. We listen to the boat's wake crash on shore until there is silence. After shouldering a knapsack full of ammunition, warm clothes, and food, I carry the 30-30 on deck and wait to be ferried ashore in an inflatable raft. When it's my turn, I drop into the raft and watch the spruce-green wall behind the beach resolve into a forest of trees as we near the sand. The boat captain warns us to be back on the beach by 3:00 p.m. That should give him enough time to reload the boat and motor us back to the Juneau dock before dark.

Bill waits for me on the sand. Together we walk down the beach and then up a narrow tidal stream. We turn our backs on the ocean's silver light and hike slowly toward a broad muskeg meadow.

✳

Dad never hunted after he gave up the 30-30. He never taught me how to stalk or kill. When a mule deer crossed in front of our family Studebaker, a gentle smile always appeared on his face. He let Walt Disney mold our attitudes about deer. Every buck I saw was Bambi's father, every doe the mother of Thumper's friend. I tried to forget about Bambi after my cousin gave me the 30-30 and the obligation not to be the one Branch who'd never bagged a deer.

✳

Bill knew about the obligation attached to my 30-30 but I also didn't know if he had ever killed a deer. None of my hunting friends talked about such things. I had no idea how many they had shot. They shared good venison recipes but never drew attention with hunting stories. Their reticence postponed the need for me to think about the kill. Would I pass the gun test? Would I find pleasure in bloodletting or just satisfy some hardwired need to kill for food? If a capacity to watch suffering from my action was required, did I have it?

I had never even pointed the rifle at a deer on earlier trips. But, during a previous hunt, I had watched a young deer fall from a bullet to the head, thrash like an epileptic on the forest floor, then run into thick woods. We all rejoiced that night after the shooter found his wounded deer and quickened its death.

✳

I never cried at my father's funeral or in the years following his death. I came close when I stumbled on a photo I took of him rowing a boat on a lake in Northern B.C. It was his face that almost turned on the tears—eyes sparkling in late afternoon light, the smile of a man sharing something wonderful with his son. We were returning to California from a road trip to Alaska. I had just graduated from Berkeley and would start law school in September. He talked a lot about retiring from his parking meter repair job. The photograph captured the contentment of a man about to climb into the Big Rock Candy Mountains. Dad, who could not stay on key, sang me that song of his childhood on the drive out of Alaska. His voice grew louder when he got to "In the Big Rock Candy Mountains all the cops have wooden legs and little streams of alcohol come trickling down the rocks..."

✳

From the cover of two-hundred-year-old spruce, Bill and I strain to spot deer on the meadow. Nothing walks among the islands of wind-tortured shore pine and mountain hemlock that dot the plain of dead-brown grass. A raven squawked just before Bill falls into a narrow but deep muskrat channel. The purple-black bird continues what now sounds like a laugh. It sits atop a tall mountain hemlock and looks into the meadow, chortling until we walk onto the muskeg. Then he flies to a twisted pine fifty yards away and starts up again.

✳

I was living in Ketchikan when I rediscovered the picture of Dad on the lake. Tired of carrying around a hard ball of unresolved grief over his death, I asked a master carver to help me use the photo as a template for a mask of my dad. I hoped that the valves frozen tight for Dad's funeral would leak grief as I watched his face emerge from a block of alder wood.

We carved in the Sensei's garage while separated by a long wooden table. The first night, I opened my canvas tool roll full of knives sharp enough to shave hair off my arm. All had been swirled over three grades of Japanese water stones and then buffed to a razor's edge with a leather strop.

Sensei looked briefly at my tool roll and then at my father's photograph. His reading glasses slid down to the tip of his nose as he studied my father's round face. He saw Dad's small oval eyes split by a curving nose with a ridge bulge. He smiled after noticing a similar bulge on my nose.

✳

We leapfrog with the raven until he settles on the top of a stunted mountain hemlock and falls silent. Thirty feet away, a young buck moves into view

Dan's carving of his father's mask

and freezes. Yup'ik men I knew in Bethel told me that seals give themselves to the honorable hunter. Is this deer giving himself to me?

✳

Sensei led me outside to pick out a suitable piece of alder wood for the mask. At his urging, I selected a round with unblemished grey and white bark. A series of perfectly symmetrical growth rings radiated out from its center. I split the round in two with an axe, chipped away the bark from a half-round and carried it into the shop. In benediction of my choice, Sensei set aside the other half-round for a future project.

The wood came from a spring fallen tree, cut while sap flowed up from the roots so it smelled of green growth and unfurling leaves. Moisture sprayed out with every adze blow, some striking my face. Without being told, I used my straight blade adze to turn the half-round of firewood into a rectangle and drew the rough shape of my father's head onto the top plane.

✳

Until today, I had never looked into a deer's eye. Did the guys who turned deer into table meat ever stop to study one of these deep brown globes? I see intelligence—an awareness of life not unlike what I see in Bill's eyes. Is it a mirror?

✳

Years after the hunt, after piecing together the evidence, I now think that my father saw an awareness of life in the eye of the last elk he hunted or maybe the mix of fear and resolution that glared out of the refugees' eyes that he captured in his photographs. Did his war rob him of the ability to take any life, even that of a forest animal? What of Otello? Dad saved the opera program, even autographed it. It lay boxed near his war photographs and his bronze star until I found it postmortem. He carried it in his tunic back from the opera house, pushing past bars and whorehouses, past the bomb-damaged homes. Can a Verdi aria, heard in a time of war, take the killing out of a man?

✻

It's easy to chip wood from a wet piece of alder but it doesn't hold the fine detail needed to finish a portrait mask. You form the geography of the face first and hollow out the back until the mask is thin enough to dry without cracking. Then you let it dry before bringing it to life with small, sharp blades.

When a crude ghost of my father's face appeared on the mask, I turned it over and used a curved blade adze to hollow out the back. I'd seen master carvers hold a mask in their laps during this step, but I placed Dad on a soft red cedar chopping block. Chips and water flew into my face as I adzed with my head bent over the inverted mask, careful not to strike my left hand with the falling blade. After a rough bowl had formed, I nestled the head in my lap and used the "U" shaped crooked knife to dig out more wood. It was slow, tense work. I checked constantly to make sure I would not cut through to the surface. Not even the Sensei could fix Dad's face if that happened.

✻

I raise the 30-30, confident of hitting my deer. Near the beach, another rifle fires but my deer does not move. I wrap my finger around the "C" shaped trigger, control my breath, aim at the heart, and lower the gun. The deer walks away.

✻

Feeling strong, I cut alder without asking for advice. Sensei saw the damage and reminded me it was only wood. I watched his sharp knives bring a reprieve, tried to ignore the reading glasses sliding to the tip of his nose, tried to forgive myself for the mistake, tried not to hate him for making that part of the mask belong to someone else. I said nothing because only he could make it good enough.

❋

Bill watched the deer ease into cover behind a confusion of mountain hemlocks. He didn't raise his own rifle or even ask me "Why?" We crossed the muskeg meadow in silence broken only by the sloppy pop our boots made when jerked free after each step on the boggy ground. I can't remember what we talked about on the beach while we waited to be ferried back to the Seasport.

❋

Months of carving had almost freed my father from excess alder. I felt the pressure and kept to shallow cuts, crosschecking often with Dad's photo. Knowing that king salmon were already feeding off of Mt. Point, Sensei took back the mask and slashed wood until shavings covered the floor. Again, I started to hate him for the violence and his ability to see my father's face in the patterned wood. When the mask returned, it had pencil guidelines for putting in his eyes. I softened knowing that he had left me the power to capture my father's kind countenance.

I finished the mask several months later during king salmon season.

❋

I feel guilt and frustration on the boat ride home from Admiralty. If I can't drop a deer that offers me such a sure shot, I'll never be able to use my father's 30-30 to take one. Bill still hasn't asked me why I didn't take the easy shot even though he knows about my obligation to my cousin.

I loved carrying the gun through woods gone to rest after the salmon runs, moving slowly, looking for the flickering ear, listening for the crack of a twig. But now I may never again stalk through forests of tall hemlock trees while fat flakes of snow settle over highbush cranberries and the thick moss that forms an electric green carpet.

❋

Even though I never saw Dad rub down the 30-30's barrel with oil or touch a sharp knife to alder wood, the smell of alder sap or gun oil still brings him to mind. Long after I last wiped it off my hands, the smell of the oil makes me think of the man who inspired the mask: the gentle one who rowed me across an unnamed British Columbia lake while still excited by Alaska, the boy who learned from a trapper how to hunt, the discharged soldier who abandoned the 30-30—my father who had refused to kill again or teach me how to hunt.

My cousin, who learned to kill deer and elk from his father with the 30-30, never went to war. He left his Idaho home to bring me the rifle. But he never thought to ask why the father who raised me gave away the gun.

Melting Ice

On the Saturday after Thanksgiving in 1976, when I was 25 years old, I walked past the corrugated-steel sides of J.B. Crowe's cold storage to where a forest of willows touched the Kuskokwim River near Bethel. Inch-long hoarfrost feathers covered the dormant willow branches. Even now, forty-five years later, I remember the sun's glare and how it brightened the frost on the dead brown willows. Hoarfrost also sparkled on salmon drift nets spread over fish racks on the other side of the frozen river. The prior night's light dusting of frost covered the dark river ice.

A hatless Yup'ik man in Converse tennis shoes, jeans, LA Lakers' sweatshirt and backpack carried three long willow poles across the new ice. His shoes left tracks in the river's surface frost. The man chopped a hole in the ice. My memory could be snatching details of his appearance from encounters with different subsistence hunters or fishermen who helped me survive years on the river or used my services as a lawyer. But, I know that a cutting blade forged from a car spring had been lashed to one of his poles. My father would have made his own ice pick blade from a car spring rather than waste money on store bought. He had always found a way to make the abandoned useful.

I hid my admiration for my father, not out of meanness, but because it made him uncomfortable. He taught me that men who fixed things hide their emotion so that is what I did on the Kuskokwim, starting with the fear I felt at the ice's edge. My father never cried. Even if I could have, I would have done it in private. Did I refrain out of fear of ridicule like that visited on me by the nuns at my Catholic grade school when I cried or because I modeled myself after a man who never showed emotion?

On the ice, I looked over at the Yup'ik man rather than down where the cold Kuskokwim moved beneath thin ice and ignored the whip-snap sound of cracks following every footstep. *That guy wouldn't be out here if it weren't safe.*

The iceman had thick, carefully combed black hair. Red frostbite scars tattooed his prominent cheeks. A network of wrinkles radiated out from the corners of his eyes. He smiled a greeting but didn't say anything. I had a camera but was afraid to take his picture. While he worked, I scuffed frost off the surface and was surprised to see gray air bubbles that had been trapped by the fast forming ice. My shadow obscured what swam beneath the bubbles.

The man chopped six holes and using a willow pole like a sewing needle, strung the line between the outmost ones. He tied the top and bottom edges of a shallow, thirty-foot-long monofilament gill net to one of the poles. Because it knows what I want, memory tells me that the man asked that I hold the net underwater with one pole while he plunged the pole tied to the other end into the water. Ice quickly reformed in the holes to keep the poles in place.

"What are you fishing for?"

"Lush."

"Ah," I said even through the only lushes I had known hung out at the bars near my San Francisco law school. Later, I learned that "lush" was the Yup'ik name for the cod-like freshwater burbot. After my first winter on the river, I appreciated the ugly fish's rich flavor.

As the ice clears and thins with age, I can no longer bury grief. Now, almost forty-five years later, the mental columbarium I constructed to niche painful memories softens and clouds like ice during the spring melt, releases remembrances of the river long ago buried in self-defense. I am learning how to cry.

✳

Because it was the only radio station in Bethel, KYUK provided the soundtrack for my waking life. Everyone listened to a public message service called "*The Tundra Drums*," and to the news read in English and Yup'ik:

"To Mary in Bethel, from Zack in Mountain Village: Please come home. The kids miss you. Don't forget the seal oil at Auntie's."

"Today searchers found the body of a the 43-year-old school teacher who died from hypothermia while trying to walk home in forty-below weather after his snowmachine broke down. He succumbed within a quarter mile from village school."

"From the VD clinic to the following people . . .Your test results are in. Please schedule an appointment by calling . . ."

"A Johnson River family grieves the loss of their four-year-old son who died after being mauled when he wandered into a sled dog yard. The child was flown to Bethel and pronounced dead by doctors at the hospital."

"Happy birthday, Evon, from Sophie and Mom and Pop."

"Yesterday, the empty boat of a Kuskokwim River man was found circling just below Steamboat Slough. The owner had been seen drinking in Bethel earlier in the day. This morning his body was found tangled in a downriver set net. He was not wearing a life jacket..."

I didn't know Evon, Mary, Zack, the deceased, or their grieving families, so I easily separated myself from their deaths like I did the deaths of other strangers on the river. My job as a lawyer, which required professional distance from my clients' grief, helped. I let the news of tragedies blend together like reports from a distant war correspondent. Each of these grief-worthy events cast a small shadow that the young man who first walked onto river ice could ignore. Today, I wonder if those shadows have congealed together, cancer-like, under the ice.

✳

My first year in the Legal Services Office, a man I'll call Sam, a VISTA volunteer lawyer from Minnesota, died at 24 of the sudden onset of pneumonia. He finished the workday on Friday, was refused admittance by the Indian Health Service Hospital on Saturday, and died Sunday. We split up his caseload on Monday. Sam's parents settled their wrongful death suit against the Indian Health Service, whose failure to provide medical care had led to their son's death.

The death should have scared me. Sam was fit. I was doughy. After work, he ran laps in the National Guard Armory gym while I rushed home to eat ice cream and watch PBS TV shows. Since it had a monopoly on medical care in Bethel, I'd be taken to the Indian Health Service Hospital if I fell ill or through the ice. Would they refuse to admit me like they had Sam? But I ignored the health risk like I refused to grieve each time I walked by Sam's empty office. I kept emotion out of my voice while explaining to Sam's clients why they had a new lawyer.

✳

On a still-dark Monday morning at the office, I learned that the troopers had arrested a friend I will call Sinka, a sweet man who had taken my law class at the college. While home in his village and drunk, he had beaten his wife to death. I can see both of their smiles, hear their laughs, but cannot imagine him in prison as someone else raises their children.

I wanted to believe, like many on the river, that ghosts of violence and perversion floated in some bottles of bootlegged whiskey; it was just bad luck that Sinka had bought one tainted by jealous anger. The judge could not allow Sinka to blame the whiskey. If valid, that legal defense would have emptied the jail in a place where alcohol is involved in almost every crime. In 1977, alcohol was a factor in all but one of the serious crimes committed in Bethel area villages surveyed by the University of Alaska's Criminal Justice Center.

In the rare criminal case without alcohol, the victim might turn to the jury and whisper, "He hit me even he was sober." A conviction was sure to follow.

It did not matter that Sinka worked hard, went to church, learned from an elder how to take his first seal, how to share it in the Yup'ik tradition. It didn't matter that I liked him, that many others did. No number of character witnesses could have saved him from jail. He had twisted off the bottle cap, poured himself a drink, downed it and then another. The law held him responsible for all that followed. Our legislators told us they were being tough on crime when they passed a law that prevented Sinka from arguing that he was innocent because booze prevented him from realizing he was killing his wife. I accepted the lawmakers' logic at the time. But now I believe that society doesn't need protection from Sinka or most of his cellmates, if they keep sober. The law didn't deter them from opening the bottle. The law is tough on the Sinkas, but not on crime.

I never lost a friend this way, but sometimes after the river firmed with ice, a person might freeze to death on a stumble home from the bootlegger's house. The next day someone, maybe a child on the way to school, might find the stiff body, often next to an empty booze bottle and the warm clothes discarded when hypothermia completed alcoholic confusion. The shock at hearing news of such a death within a few feet of warmth and safety made me click off the radio, but not before an emotionally charged memory of the death slipped beneath the ice. Now, when I read that someone in Anchorage or in one of the Western Alaska villages died from alcohol-related hypothermia, I try to match the dead person's name to families I knew. Relieved if memory can't make a match, I linger in the past for a while and remember drinking tea with a friend from the village where the person froze to death, maybe reaching for a strip of dry fish to dip into crystal-clear seal oil while the Christmas greeting show on KYUK played in the background:

"We have Eva from Kwethluk on the phone. Eva, who do you want to wish Merry Christmas to?"

"Hi. Ummmmmmm. I want to wish Merry Christmas and Happy Slavic to all my cousins in Akiak and Bethel, you know who, and to my Auntie in Aniak and all those upriver people. Why don't you ever come for a visit? Merry Christmas anyway and to Billy in Anchorage who promised he'd be home for Slavic this time."

Why do I have to work harder to remember the happier times?

My memory doesn't have to multiply the suicides to touch me with sadness. *The Tundra Drums* newspaper in Bethel reported each death of an unnamed teenager but not why the suicide chose the void of death over life; what drove away hope and the desire to live; how the child could tie the noose, slip it around the neck, kick over the chair. Alcohol might have clouded the suicide's life, rendered his parents absent or violent, and fueled wild parties that kept him sleepless with fear. Suicide in Alaska is a problem unsolved today. The rate among young Alaska Native males is still seven times higher than for other Americans.

On the river, you didn't have to be an Alaskan Native to have a drinking problem that fueled violence. At an end of a summer dinner party, I greeted a tall white guy at the door with, "Hope you are hungry because we cooked up a lot of food for everyone." Bob, physically hardened by construction work, lifted a half-gallon bottle of sour mash whiskey and said, "I'm having this for dinner." Quashing down an uneasy feeling, I stepped aside so he could enter.

After washing dishes in the kitchen, I sat next to a carpenter from Ireland's County Donegal while he instructed me in the intricacies of the Irish fight for independence, "You see Dan, O'Connell was a greatly misunderstood man, sure he was . . ." Before I could learn the true nature of the liberator, Bob interrupted with, "You see that guy over there. I am going to kill him." His face and voice showed no humor as his intended victim chortled at a joke. Hoping to avoid a violent class clash, I asked Bob to come outside where he could have a smoke. There, we shivered in shirtsleeves.

"Do you know the guy?"

"No."

"Do you even know his name?"

"Don't need to."

"Why do you want to kill him?"

"Can't stand the way he laughs."

"What about your job?"

"We're done for the year."

To distract the whiskey drinker until his intended victim left the party, I bored him with a long explanation about how I grew the broccoli and potatoes for the night's dinner in Kuskokwim River silt mixed with aged tundra peat. To avoid judging him, I blamed the whiskey for his threatening words.

I'll make a construct out of some of my clients for Mr. and Mrs. Wolfe.

The Wolfes fly into Bethel from their Yukon River village to meet their lawyer. I offer them tea or coffee. Since they live in a traditional Yup'ik village, I wait for them to speak first. Looking at the floor, Mrs. Wolfe breaks a long silence by asking when they will get their kids back. Feeling like a doctor delivering bad news in a hospital waiting room, I explain how courts work. I don't show them the trooper's pictures of their daughter's injuries but do say that Mrs. Wolfe's brother confessed to sexually penetrating the child. Neither of them responds when I say, "He told the troopers that you knew."

I promise I will try to get the kids back, being careful not to raise false expectations. I ask if they have any relatives the kids could stay with until the case runs its course. Then they realize that I have no power or magic wand and hope drains away.

I can still remember the signs—a softening of their faces, veils of moisture forming over irises, a sudden contraction of face muscles, then tears.

I look away to study the police report just before the tears. I stay shallow and bury my fear of failing them. I push hard at court, try to use cross-examination questions to soften the expert's negative testimony and cloud the memory of fact witnesses. Alcohol treatment counselors pass on the Wolfes' promises to work the recovery program and keep their kids safe. I do my job, with as much zeal as I can muster, try not to take responsibility for win or loss. The Wolfes lose. After court, I drop their file in the "to be closed" pile and try to forget everything in it—to slide the Wolfes and their problems beneath the ice so I can maintain professional distance when the next client walks through the law office door.

Some of the Bethel bar softened their court memories with whiskey, beer, or wine. Fearing my clients' fate, I burned off my stress behind a small dog team. A circle of eight sled dogs surrounded our house on 6th Avenue. They barked and yelped on my approach after a day in court, as if driving off ghosts. Frenzied by the idea of running, a black bloodhound mix named Rufus clamped his teeth onto his plywood doghouse and waved it in the air. I always hooked him last to the sled. Otherwise, he would chew through the gangline that attached the dogs to the sled. By then, all the dogs were leaping and straining to pull the sled loose from its anchor so they could fly down the trail. If the noise hadn't banished all the sad memories under the ice, the delicious terror I felt standing on the sled runners did. Trying to stay shallow, I pulled the quick release and we bounced out of the back yard in sudden silence. Usually, I was still on the back of the sled when the dogs had slowed to a manageable speed.

✣

The situation was better in Aniak. My wife and I moved to that upriver village of three hundred after ending our ten-year stay in Bethel. At that point, I could no longer handle the emotional stress from child protection or child sexual abuse cases. The village had less bootlegged booze and violence. Like Bethel, it was a border town where Yup'ik culture intersects mainstream America's. The high school kids adopted the nickname "Half-breeds" in proud acceptance of their mixed Yup'ik and European ancestry.

My job as village magistrate required a disinterested outsider, one known not to take sides. Without the need to maintain a lawyer's professional distance, my memory hasn't clouded over as much of my Aniak history. I married couples, sentenced the convicted, and served as coroner. Since I was a fulltime referee rather than legal counselor, no one spoke to me in confidence of their wrongdoings or even shared village gossip.

My first day as a magistrate, I found three coroner files on my desk. Each described the alcohol-related suicide of a different young man. Police and medical examiner reports, with their dry descriptions of blood splatter, shot patterns, and alcohol blood content dulled the images but I had enough imagination and experience from interviewing victims or witnesses of tragedy to paint the back story of death in each case.

In my mind, I see one of the suicides. In his early 20's, he slumps despondent about something, maybe over having spent his childhood at his local school to prepare for a life unavailable in the village, wasting the period of his life that his grandfather had spent learning from an elder how to hunt, fish, survive in the woods. I see him drain the bootlegged whiskey bottle, stretch out on his cot with a loaded shotgun on his chest, pull the trigger, not delayed by thought.

I can see the face of the mother as she answers a gray-haired trooper's death investigation questions. Reticent to talk even with the people she loves about the alcohol-driven suicide of her son, she reluctantly answers the questions of the uniformed white man. She saw no other choice. He had sent her son's body to Anchorage to be carved open like a moose. He had the power to arrest and take others away.

"Was he unhappy?"

"Sometimes."

"Was he drinking long before he died?"

"Maybe."

"Did he often keep to himself–stay away?"

"Ii I, I mean yes."

"Do you know why he killed himself?"

"No."

I imagine the interview taking place at the kitchen table in one of the little log houses they build in that village. An icon or holy card of a favorite saint occupies wall space just above the mother's head. Mugs of coffee cool on the table. The trooper uses his quiet voice, each sentence softer than the prior one, sensitive to the way the mother flinches at each question. He leans very close to her face as he strains to hear her soft responses. The interview ends with the trooper's last gulp of coffee.

At least that death involved alcohol, allowing the survivors something to blame for the loss of their father, uncle, brother, son, grandson—the man who repaired the house and brought them moose meat, fish, firewood, love. The parents of sober children who killed themselves didn't even have this. They could, though, grieve at Yup'ik wakes.

A professional outsider, I never attended a Yup'ik wake. I have been told that the body, usually in an open wooden box, sits on two sawhorses in the largest room. People bring food to share, fish-head and rice soup or moose stew, if someone had just shot one. Others bring dried salmon and seal oil for dipping. Kind even in mourning, the family welcome visitors to take one of the chairs near the body and share a last supper with the one who died. A family elder comforts those who cry.

Does my memory exaggerate the numbers of tragic deaths on the river because I tried to ignore them and the sadness because back then I refused to grieve even for the ones I had known alive? I buried grief for the dead or imprisoned with the memories of police reports, run-ins with drunks, social worker reports, and testimony of child victims. But, I never sought relief at a Yup'ik wake, even when assured that I was welcome. Instead, I rationalized that I could not impose on people who could not afford to be generous with their time, food, or kindness. They shared these things with people who came to the river for money, not to help or learn, and who left to spend their gain in the Lower 48 states. The people of the river would have shared with me. My real reason may have been fear—of being seen as foolish, of saying or doing the wrong thing, of my first adult tears, of the burden that would come if I crossed the line from neighbor to friend, from friend to family. At each chance to heal, I stepped back.

✳

During the first years on the river, I tried to ignore needless death, refused to share my feelings about those deaths that I could not ignore. I was there to help the river people. But my work as a defense attorney or child protection lawyer sometimes placed victims at risk. Most on the river showed me kindness and welcome. When the troopers arrested someone for an act of drunken violence who had showed me kindness, like Sinka, I wanted to blame the alcohol he drank, not the person buying the bottle. I wanted to blame the bootlegger, the white village schoolteachers who punished his parents for speaking Yup'ik in school, even God for allowing it to happen. After a few years, when I convinced myself that only the drinker could stop the drinking, I had to blame Sinka and consider his prison sentence necessary. There seemed no other choice since I lived in a land full of kind loving people, more than a few who couldn't avoid violence if they drank. As I worked in a system that stuffed the jail beyond capacity with nice guys when sober, I barricaded myself from their pain. Today, knowing that the number of criminal defense lawyers in Bethel has multiplied since my time on the river, I circle back to blame the booze but can't think of a way to stem the violence.

＊

I still like leaning into a cold wind like the ones that always swept across Bethel in winter. I enjoyed the harsh challenge of the river and my life there. The Yup'ik people kept me twelve years on a river that offered little physical beauty. When years after leaving the Kuskokwim, I meet friends from the river in Anchorage or Juneau, they act like I am on a long vacation from Bethel, like I still live in their world.

I wonder if someone more empathic than I would have lasted as long on the river or still be homesick for it when sandhill cranes, an icon of Southwest Alaska, fly over his rainforest home. Perhaps my old ability to bury emotions allows me to love it even now. I have white friends who never built a barrier between themselves and the river people. They went to fish camps, took part in hunting trips, attended Yup'ik funerals and wakes. They cherish rather than fear their memories. But few of them were lawyers submerged in cases where a nice person when sober got drunk and raped a neighbor or allowed unspeakable things to happen to children.

＊

During a recent walk near Juneau with another Bethel exile, I remembered a young woman from a lower Yukon River village. An orphan, she had been beautiful and kind. A wave of sadness distorted the words I used to ask if he remembered her death in the village. Tears wet my eyes as he answered, "Yes."

The troopers found her body among those of passed-out men and women. She and the others lay like severed flower petals around a washtub of homebrew. When woken by the troopers, none of the living remembered the woman being raped with a fireplace poker or knew that she had bled to death from her wounds.

I was surprised that a 30-year-old death could bring tears. I never cried during my river years—not for Sinka, suicides, or even the abused children. I should have expected the tears. When I couldn't slide sadness under the ice while writing child protection briefs for the Alaska Supreme Court, I should have expected future fracturing.

The young man who walked out of California and onto the Kuskokwim River ice could not have cried. The nuns made the act shameful. Later he refrained out of ignorance. Not understanding the mechanics of sorrow, he was afraid that the tears might never stop—that he might never be able to take on the legal case of another person who endured pain or who caused sorrow.

You Can't Go Home Again

Over thirty-four years ago, Susan and I loaded our skiff and moved 130 miles up the Kuskokwim River to Aniak. We have moved two more times since and now live in Juneau, a thousand miles away from where we launched the skiff. After we left, the State, Federal and Tribal governments poured millions of dollars into Bethel. The population doubled.

When we arrived in Bethel during the mid-70s, about 3,000 people lived in that Kuskokwim River town. We all slept in houses or shacks connected to the town's small power grid. But few of us had flush toilets or even running water. Neither Susan nor I would live in a house with a flush toilet until our last year in Aniak. The insulation in Susan's Mission Road house was almost nonexistent. During cold winter days, she had to stand on a kitchen chair to keep her feet from freezing when she was on the phone

If Yup'ik people hadn't shared kindness and humor during our twelve-and-a-half-year stay on the Kuskokwim River, nothing would have stirred my longing to return. That longing blossomed in 2004, after I was interviewed by members of the Judicial Council for a Juneau District Court judge job. Seconds after the interview began, I knew that I had no chance. One of the council members even called me a weak candidate because I lacked jury trial experience. He was wrong.

I had done a lot of jury work as a defense attorney and magistrate in Bethel and Aniak. In one jury trial, I had represented an immigrant

accused of committing more than twenty felonies, including at least one assault with a deadly weapon charge. A good judge would have told the Council that at the end of the state's case, my client was allowed to plead guilty to misdemeanor Assault in a Fourth Degree charge in exchange for dismissal, with prejudice, of all the other charges.

Alex Bryner, then the Chief Justice of the Alaska Supreme Court, was a member of the Judicial Council. When the interview ended, he thanked me for sharing a little legal history of my time on the Kuskokwim River. Then, he encouraged me to apply for an open Superior Court judge job in Bethel.

That evening, I told Susan in an excited voice about Justice Bryner's suggestion. She smiled and said, "It will be a long commute." I had temporarily forgotten that our daughter was then a sophomore at Juneau Douglas High School. We couldn't ask her to give up her friends and teachers here and start again in Bethel. Susan saw no reason for me to abandon my solid assistant attorney general job in Juneau for a judge position in Bethel, even though we'd be moving to the town where we first met and fell in love.

Any thought that we would return to Bethel quickly faded as I settled back into my life at the Attorney General's Office. My caseload, which included work on state legislation, kept me happy in Juneau.

Years later, on a wet Juneau morning in November, I learned that the child protection attorneys in Bethel needed someone to cover their cases while they spent the Christmas holiday with families in the Lower 48. Before leaving the Kuskokwim River town, I had represented many parents in Child in Need of Aid court cases. In Ketchikan, I switched sides and represented social workers in the same kind of litigation. The supervisor of the Bethel child protection team quickly accepted my offer to cover their caseload during the week before Christmas.

In late December, the Bethel sun, when not blocked by storm clouds, cut a low arc across the winter sky. It rose above the tundra around 11 A.M. and dropped back beneath it five and a half hours later. At that time of the year, it never provided warmth. I knew all this and still boarded a plane to Bethel.

A Korean taxi driver took me from the Bethel Airport to a large and rambling bed and breakfast just across the street from the Kuskokwim River. I carried my suitcase and a three-quarter sized guitar toward the B and B, slammed snow off my boots in the arctic entry way, and entered the lobby. As I used my handkerchief to wipe clouds of fog off my glass lens, a lovely sounding Yup'ik woman called out my name, like she would have if we were old friends. I would have found this odd in any other B and B. But Yup'ik people keep old memories of those they knew on the Kuskokwim. Maybe she had one of me.

After my glasses defrosted, I still could not recognize the woman who had called out a welcome. She certainly didn't know me. She hadn't been born before Susan and I moved to Aniak. With four or five questions, I could have discovered the name of her village, parents, cousins, and siblings. Instead of using that interrogation technique, I just followed her through a winding hall way to the little room I would sleep in for the rest of week.

I loved meeting the Yup'ik woman, like I enjoyed running into Bethel people while working in Anchorage. Once, years after I moved away from the Kuskokwim, I met one on 4th Avenue after flying from Juneau to Anchorage for court.

While thinking about my upcoming court hearing, I heard someone with a male Yup'ik accent shout "Hi Dan." We both stopped and smiled. Then we joined our right hands and lifted them once up and down, like

Yup'ik people do in the Yukon-Kuskokwim Delta. He asked if I still lived in my old house on Bethel's Sixth Avenue. He said that he hadn't been past that place since he and his family moved to Anchorage many years ago. The man didn't seem shocked when I told him when Susan and I had moved away. Maybe he was teasing me, like he did so well when we both lived in Bethel.

The next morning, I wandered into the B and B's dining room where the same Yup'ik woman was setting out milk, cereal, and toast. I was the only one there wearing a tie. The other tenants wore Carhart pants and heavy, long sleeved shirts even though they'd be driving around all day in well heated trucks. They must have believed that I would freeze to death if I tried to walk to the courthouse in the casual court clothes I was wearing.

After breakfast, I pulled my old Walls Blizzard Proof snowmachine suit over my court clothes. It had kept me warm in 1984 when I ran the Kuskokwim 300. I only used it in Juneau when Taku winter winds hammered the downtown streets.

I don't remember being slammed by cold winter air when I started walking to court. But I do know that in seconds frost clouded over my glasses. I slipped them into one of my shirt pockets and continued half-blind along the frozen river. Then the wind rose. Fortunately, I was wearing a beaver hat that a Bethel seamstress made for me in 1976. The woolen scarf that I had wrapped around the lower half of my face protected me from frostbite.

I should have had been miserable walking to the courthouse. But I felt like I had been invited to a family reunion. I leaned into the wind, like I had leaned into the wind every winter morning when walking to my Bethel law office.

Trudging along a snowmachine trail that crossed Mission Road, I neared Watson's Corner, the only major intersection in Bethel, where the Chief Eddie Hoffman Road bends north toward the high school and the Alaska State Housing Authority subdivision. Another road branched off to the northeast to deliver families to Kilbuck School.

In less than a minute I managed to climb the icy side of Chief Eddie's road but an unbroken vehicle chain prevented me from crossing it. When

I lived in Bethel, the traffic was always light. This morning, a long line of cars and pickup trucks stretched out beyond the hospital. None of the drivers stopped to let me cross the road. They needed to keep moving so they could drop off their kids at school before the start of classes.

A city truck passed by, trying to cover the icy road with a layer of fine sand. But, the wind carried off the grit before it could settle onto the ice.

I stood on the road's edge for ten minutes. Finally, one of the trucks slowed enough for me to make it to the other side. In a few more minutes I reached the new courthouse/law office complex. The front door was still locked even though it was past the normal opening time of 8 A.M. I had a key but no cigarette lighter to melt the ice from the lock's key slot. A lighter was always required to open the Legal Services office door on winter mornings. But that day, the door opened after I inserted and twisted the courthouse key.

I could hear men talking about criminal cases when I passed the District Attorney's Office. No one came out to say "hi." Later in the day, I walked over to courthouse portion of the building and appeared in some child protection proceedings. The Yup'ik woman who served as magistrate did a good job conducting the hearings. Did she realize that I knew her Yup'ik mother before she passed away and spent many hours appearing in cases before the Superior Court judge who fathered her?

It took me awhile to accept that almost all those I appeared before or with that week were either tiny children or just dreams in their parents' minds when I lawyered in Bethel and served as a magistrate in Aniak. But that didn't prevent them from showing me respect and kindness, the things that they do for elders.

I was pleased by the kind treatment they showed me, but was sobered by how many things had changed at the courthouse since I moved to Southeast Alaska, to say nothing of the town. When Susan and I lived in Bethel, the court house was part of the City Office Building. Few lawyers owned a car, so those of us unwilling to take a taxi walked to court on dirt trails in cold or wet weather. We always had to arrive early so we would have enough time to pull off our weather gear and put on a tie.

That night I had dinner in a Korean restaurant and then walked back to the B and B. Since no one seemed to be using any of the nearby rooms,

I tuned up my guitar and started stumbling through Bach's "Jesu, Joy of Man's Desiring." Then I played his "Sleepers, Wake." Outside my room, someone scaped a chair across the floor. I stopped playing and opened the door. The beautiful Yup'ik woman was sitting in the hallway. She smiled and said she just wanted to hear the music.

She got the five discovery questions instead of more guitar music. Her mother and aunties were her age when I lived in Bethel. I remembered their young faces. I smiled each time she named someone I had once known and still respected.

After she left, I put away the guitar and stretched out on my bed. Reflecting on the day's experiences didn't make me smile or frown. They just reminded me that I had aged someplace else while money had poured into the village and the population grew.

When Susan and I first moved to Bethel, we knew the owner of every rig that didn't serve as a taxi. Now everyone seems to have their own car or truck. In 1977, there was only one TV station. It aired PBS shows and evening news recorded the night before in Seattle and sent north daily on a Wien Airlines jet. World Series baseball games were aired on the TV station two weeks after they were played down south.

We spent much more time visiting or being visited by friends than watching TV. They became family. They'd come to the cabin, five or six at a time, to watch a Public Television show on my six-inch-wide TV screen, tell stories, and drink hot coffee or tea. Many of those folks drifted out of our life. But, a handful are still important to us.

While my blond hair, rectangular shaped head, and blue eyes made me stand out in Bethel as a stranger in a strange land, Susan's features made her look like a hometown girl. She had thick, black hair that hung around her beautiful Japanese face. Like a Yup'ik, Susan's delicate eyes closed tight when she laughed. She always looked like a local when visiting clients, having tea with Yup'iks, or shopping at the Alaska Commercial Store.

Sometimes, a Bethel local would ask Susan if she was an Amik. A large family with that name lived in Kipnuk Village, an hour's plane ride away. When she visited other villages, people would often ask her the same question. After Susan had lived in Bethel for several years, an older Yup'ik couple walked up to her while she shopped in the AC Store. The man, who Susan could tell was Mr. Amik said, "You should come home with us."

Susan had at least one other connection with Yup'ik culture. She learned about it while attending a youth and elder conference in Bethel. The instructor told the group that Yup'ik adults teach children by telling stories rather than lecturing them. Susan remembered that her father used the same teaching approach. Rather than give her a straight answer to a question, he would tell a story. She often interrupted to demand that he just answer her question with a simple "yes" or "no." He'd just continue on until he finished the tale. The answer was always there. Susan had to wait patiently for it to appear, like Yup'ik children must do.

My wife and I loved our time on the Kuskokwim, but towards the end of this Bethel visit, I knew that I could never live on the river again. There had been too many big changes since we left. Nothing could transform Bethel back into the little village that Susan and I loved.

When we moved there, most people took cabs or walked. Now they created little traffic jams on their way to work or delivering their kids to school. We really enjoyed talking with people picking up their mail at the old downtown Post Office. Now they have to drive several miles out the road to the new one.

When living in Bethel, we learned to put up with honey bucket bathrooms, expensive groceries, and very hungry mosquitoes. I found myself loving cold winter winds, fishing salmon in summer and driving a dog team in winter. Susan and I both enjoyed the time spent with Yup'ik people in Bethel or at one of the villages. Bethelites now seem to use their time after work watching movies or cable TV shows at home.

I never mastered Yup'ik even though I took an introductory course at Kuskokwim College. But I always believed that if I listened to a Yup'ik speaker long enough, I could become one myself.

I never tired of hearing the homilies delivered in Yup'ik by deacons at Immaculate Conception Church in Bethel, Yup'ik stories shared with children, or speeches made at village conferences. We sang Yup'ik hymns at Mass and listened to drummers chant it during Yup'ik dances. At times when I miss Bethel the most, I listen to a cassette of church songs sung in the language of the Lower Kuskokwim.

I still love my memories of Bethel, but Susan and I can't move back to that river city. It and we have changed too much. It has gotten too hard for us to lean into the tundra wind.

ACKNOWLEDGMENTS

Many of the essays in this book have appeared in literary magazines. The author thanks the following journals for publishing these poems or essays: "A Little Traction" in *Slippery Elm Literary Magazine*; "Body of Christ" in *Portland Magazine*; "Dirty Work" in *Gravel*; "Dust" in *Kestrel*; "Elegy" in *Cirque*; "Following Raven" in *Concho River Review*; "Just a Ferryman" in *Hippocampus Magazine*; "My Father's Son" in *Twisted Vine Literary Journal*; "Someday I'll Miss This Place Too" in *Windfall*; "The Californian" in *Cardiff Review*; "The Fire Extinguisher" in *The Nasiona*; "The Last Seat" in *Windmill*; "The Skiff" in *Tahoma Literary Review*; "Blind Faith" and "Welcome to the Bush" in *Tidal Echoes*.

Thank you to the above-named journal publishers and the professors, mentors, and fellow students for sharing their wisdom and advice to help me produce something solid, including University of Alaska, Anchorage Professors Eva Saulitis, Nancy Lord, David Stevenson, Sherry Simpson, Richard Chiapponne, Erin Coughlin Hollowell, Jan Deblieu, Valerie Miner, Anne Caston, and Zack Rogow. Thanks also to friend and published author Doug Pope, my wife Susan, daughter Anna, and editor Michael Burwell for helping to make the essays in this book a better read.

I am also grateful to the Yup'ik people of Southwest Alaska, whose grace, kindness, and patience with my stumbling still makes me homesick for Bethel and the Kuskokwim River. Readers should understand that while many of these essays share my impressions of Southwest Alaska from 1976 until 1989 when I moved away, only the last essay tries to paint a picture of life on the river after my wife and I left.

ABOUT THE AUTHOR

Before he moved to Bethel, Alaska in 1976, Dan Branch was more likely to watch TV than write stuff for other people to read. The one poem he drafted for his high school prom date almost ended their relationship. The teacher running his high school newspaper fired him a month into the semester. Another said that his word usage was so bad, he'd have to take one writing class each college semester if he wanted to get an office job after graduation. He followed that advice, which probably helped him gain acceptance into a California law school.

Branch took a VISTA lawyer job in Bethel, which at the time had a decent library and a recently created public television station. Fearing insane-producing boredom, he brought with him an almost complete set of Russian classics. Between reading Tolstoy and working his law job, he started to journal. He lived in Bethel and Aniak for over 13 years before moving to Southeast Alaska.

During the past 25 years he has written quarterly columns for *The Alaska Bar Association Rag*, and articles for *The Anchorage Daily News*, including pieces about a Ketchikan grave digger, a chief on one of the Alaska Marine Highway ships, and a man who managed a remote salmon hatchery in Southeast Alaska. Once, one of his legal opinions was reported in newspapers in Alaska and the Lower 48 States because it declared that it was illegal for Alaskan charities to raise money by soliciting bets on rat races.

After retirement, Branch obtained an MFA degree from the University of Anchorage, Alaska. He now lives with his wife and opinionated poodle in Juneau.

ABOUT CIRQUE PRESS

Cirque Press grew out of *Cirque*, a literary journal that publishes the works of writers and artists from the North Pacific Rim, a region that reaches north from Oregon to the Yukon Territory, south through Alaska to Hawaii, and west to the Russian Far East.

Cirque Press is a partnership of Sandra Kleven, publisher, and Michael Burwell, editor. Ten years ago, we recognized that works of talented writers in the region were going unpublished, and the Press was launched to bring those works to fruition. We publish fiction, non-fiction, and poetry, and we seek to produce art that provides a deeper understanding about the region and its cultures. The writing of our authors is significant, personal, and strong.

Sandra Kleven – Michael Burwell, publishers and editors
www.cirquejournal.com

BOOKS BY CIRQUE PRESS

Apportioning the Light – Karen Tschannen (2018)

The Lure of Impermanence – Carey Taylor (2018)

Echolocation – Kristin Berger (2018)

Like Painted Kites & Collected Works – Clifton Bates (2019)

Athabaskan Fractal: Poems of the Far North – Karla Linn Merrifield (2019)

Holy Ghost Town – Tim Sherry (2019)

Drunk on Love: Twelve Stories to Savor Responsibly – Kerry Dean Feldman (2019)

Wide Open Eyes: Surfacing from Vietnam – Paul Kirk Haeder (2020)

Silty Water People – Vivian Faith Prescott (2020)

Life Revised – Leah Stenson (2020)

Oasis Earth: Planet in Peril – Rick Steiner (2020)

The Way to Gaamaak Cove – Doug Pope (2020)

Loggers Don't Make Love – Dave Rowan (2020)

The Dream That Is Childhood – Sandra Wassilie (2020)

Seward Soundboard – Sean Ulman (2020)

The Fox Boy – Gretchen Brinck (2021)

Lily Is Leaving: Poems – Leslie Ann Fried (2021)

One Headlight – Matt Caprioli (2021)

November Reconsidered – Marc Janssen (2021)

Someday I'll Miss this Place Too – Dan Branch (2021)

Out There in the Out There – Jerry McDonnell (2021)

Fish the Deep Water Hard – Eric Heyne (2021)

CIRCLES
Illustrated books from Cirque Press

Baby Abe: A Lullaby for Lincoln – Anne Chandonnet (2021)

Miss Tami, Is Today Tomorrow? – Tami Phelps (2021)

Made in the USA
Middletown, DE
15 January 2022

58737201R00117